NATIONAL INDEX OF PARISH REGISTERS

A Guide to Anglican, Roman Catholic and Nonconformist Registers before 1837, together with information on Bishop's Transcripts, modern copies and Marriage Licences.

VOLUME VI

THE NORTH MIDLANDS

PART I

STAFFORDSHIRE

Compiled by

Peter D. Bloore B.Sc., Ph.D., C.Eng., FIChem.E.

Edited by

Patrick Palgrave-Moore BA., FSA., FSG

SOCIETY OF GENEALOGISTS

37 Harrington Gardens

London SW7 4JX

1982

Published by the

Society of Genealogists

37 Harrington Gardens,

London SW7 4JX

1982

F. Crowe & Sons Ltd., 11 Concorde Road, Norwich NR6 6BJ
From originals supplied by Publisher

ISBN   0.901878. 56.1

Volumes of the National Index of Parish Registers already published:

Volume 1   General Sources of Births, Marriages and Deaths before 1837
               Parish Registers, Marriage Licences, Monumental Inscriptions
               Newspapers, Clandestine Marriages, Divorce, Mediaeval
               Sources, Other Records, General Bibliography.

Volume 2   Sources for Nonconformist Genealogy and Family History The
               Three Denominations (Presbyterians, Independents and
               Baptists), Society of Friends, Moravians, Methodists, Foreign
               Churches, Other Denominations.

Volume 3   Sources for Roman Catholic Genealogy and Family History
               with a short section of Jewish Records contributed by
               Edgar Samuel. Index to Volumes 1, 2 and 3.

Volume 4   South East England
               Kent, Surrey and Sussex.

Volume 5   South Midlands and Wels Border
               Gloucestershire, Herefordshire, Oxfordshire, Shropshire,
               Warwickshire, Worcestershire.

Volume 11   North East England
(part 1)   Durham, Northumberland.

Volume 12   Sources for Scottish Genealogy and Family History
               Historical Background, Parish Registers, Ancillary Sources,
               Nonconformists, Bibliography.

VOLUME VI

PART I

CONTENTS

STAFFORDSHIRE

PREFACE TO VOLUME VI

With the increasing deposit of registers and the growing interest in transcription the workload in preparing for publication regional volumes in this series has changed dramatically since the series was first conceived. The problems of continually updating one County list whilst work on related counties is awaited have been recognised and the Society has agreed to consider the publication of individual counties as part of regional volumes to avoid the risk of such delays undermining the whole project.

Staffordshire is the first County to benefit from this decision and it is hoped that publishing now will give an added impetus not only to those currently working on the remaining counties in this region, Nottinghamshire and Derbyshire but also to those working on individual counties previously held back through lack of interest from their neighbouring counties.

Although some work on Staffordshire was commenced over a decade ago, the change in the location of archive material and the growth in transcribed copies has necessitated a fresh start here. This has been admirably undertaken by Peter Bloore whose work follows closely along the lines laid down in the regional volume for South East England.

GENERAL INTRODUCTION TO THE SERIES

The series of volumes of which this forms part evolved from a plan of Mr. J.S.W. Gibson to prepare a new edition of the <u>National Index of Parish Register Copies</u> last published by the Society of Genealogists in 1939. His idea was to arrange the work by county with each parish listed, whether or not copies of the registers had been made, and not in one alphabetical sequence as previously.

The plan developed into a series of regional volumes, listing under each parish within counties, the extent of coverage and the whereabouts of the original parish registers, register copies and bishops transcripts. In addition general information was to be given for each county on record repositories, nonconformity, marriage licences, regimental records, monumental inscriptions, newspapers and local societies.

The early history of the series is set out adequately in Volume I, pages ix-xi. From this it will be seen that by 1966 work on nearly all the regional volumes was at an advanced stage. In that year Volume V was published covering the counties of Gloucestershire, Herefordshire, Oxfordshire, Shropshire, Warwickshire and Worcestershire.

In the following ten years work on the series progressed steadily. However, despite the indefatigable work of Mr. D.J. Steel, Mr. J.S.W. Gibson and others, many factors prevented any one regional volume reaching publication. The foundation of the Federation of Family History Societies and the subsequent emergence of a national network of local family history and genealogical societies greatly increased work on register transcription. The Genealogical Society of the Church of Jesus Christ of Latter-Day Saints had greatly increased its library/holdings in Salt Lake City by an extensive programme of microfilming parish registers in this country. As a result of local government boundary changes in 1974 many deposited parish registers were transferred to other record offices. At the same time these repositories were experiencing a new wave of deposits of parochial records from local incumbents.

By the time I took over the editorship of the series it was obvious that much of the work previously done was so outdated that a fresh start had to be made. Work was re-commenced on counties with comparatively recent listings in the hope that a greater concentration of activity would ensure early publication.

Many of the registers and bishops transcripts filmed by the Genealogical Society of the Church of Jesus Christ of Latter-Day Saints were indexed by them into their Computer File Index. In 1977 printouts from this in the form of microfiche became available in many national and regional societies and libraries. However, as the Computer File Index covers records already surveyed, details of the various holdings of microfiche by these libraries are not being included in this series.

In 1978 the General Synod of the Church of England passed the Parochial Registers and Records Measure making compulsory the deposit of parish records in diocesan record offices unless certain safeguarding conditions were met in the church. The notice of this Measure coming at the same time as an increase in the spate of church thefts, only quickened the gathering momentum of deposits, making work on updating the Index a major task. Recognising that the lists might become rapidly outdated the Society, however, felt that a cut-off date had to be imposed. Consequently these movements must be borne in mind although the editor is making every effort to ensure that each volume is up to date at the time of publication.

Patrick Palgrave-Moore
Editor, 1979.

GENERAL INFORMATION

The following words of explanation about the contents of the National Index series as a whole may be helpful.

The county prefaces include information on Record Repositories, Original Registers, Bishops Transcripts. Modern Copies, Marriage Indexes, Marriage Licences, Nonconformist and Catholic Registers, Regimental Registers, pre-1837 Newspapers, Publishing Societies, other local Societies and a Bibliography.

Parish Registers

The basic aim has been to cover only registers dating before 1837. Parishes founded after 1837 have therefore not normally been entered, unless they were previously chapelries of another parish and kept separate registers. However, where the registers of pre-1837 parishes have been deposited at a County Record Office or elsewhere, the terminal dates are given even if these are long after 1837, but of course deposited registers of parishes formed after 1837 have not been included, an illogical but unavoidable distinction. In the case of Original Registers still with the incumbent, the starting dates are normally given with a + sign meaning "onwards". In practice this invariably means "beyond 1837". In the case of Original Registers, but not Bishop's Transcripts it normally indicates that entries continue from the date listed up to the present.

It is important to remember that the index gives only a summary of the registers. Duplicate and overlapping registers have therefore normally been ignored. An effort has been made to include registers of Banns, but returns made for the National Register of Archives or completed circulars have often been deficient in that respect and no guarantee can be made that where no Banns register is listed, one does not exist. The dates given for Banns include all Banns whether they are in a separate register or in a combined register with the marriages.

Bishop's Transcripts

The amount of information it has been possible to include with regard to the Bishop's Transcripts varies considerably from county to county. This is partly because many records have not been fully sorted and listed and partly because the degree of completeness of the Transcripts themselves varies. In some counties it has been possible to show every missing year. In others only four year gaps have been noted and in others only ten year gaps. In the case of one or two counties, such as Gloucestershire, the only information given is the date of the first transcript. It is most important that users of this index should read the section on Bishop's Transcripts in the relevant County preface to familiarise themselves with the degree of detail recorded for that particular county.

When the + sign is used after Bishop's Transcript dates, it indicates that the transcripts continue beyond 1837, but unlike Parish Registers, it must be borne in mind that they do not normally continue beyond the 19th Century.

Modern Copies

An attempt has been made to include all known copies whether Printed, Typescript, Manuscript, Photostat or Microfilm in libraries and record repositories in England and Wales. Repositories outside England and Wales have not normally been included with the solitary exception of the Genealogical Society of Utah in Salt Lake City, whose collection is so vast that American users of this book may find it handy to have some indication that there is a copy there. However, a word of warning is necessary. The Church is microfilming registers and Bishop's Transcripts at such a rate that if no copy at Salt Lake City is listed it does not necessarily mean that one does not exist. Any list including Mormon material is bound to be out of date before it is printed.

In the case of a printed volume it may be assumed that there is a copy in the British Library and, unless otherwise stated, in the Society of Genealogists' Library. There is normally also a copy at Salt Lake City. However, in the case of Durham and Northumberland the Society of Genealogists does not have complete sets of all the volumes printed. Except in the case of very rare books it may safely be assumed that the County Library has a copy and more often than not, the County Record Office.

Every attempt has been made to keep the list of typescript and manuscript copies up to date and as regards copies in the Society of Genealogists' Library, each county list is up to date at the time of going to press. In the case of other libraries and repositories however, it has not been possible to recircularize them all, so it is quite possible that copies deposited recently may not have been included.

In using modern copies the attention of readers is drawn to the general article on the subject which points out some of the many pitfalls. In compiling the index every effort has been made to overcome one of these - the possibility that the "copy" may consist of extracts only. Every parish register copy in the Society of Genealogists' library has been examined to check on this, and this point was emphasized in the questionnaires sent out to libraries. Normally extracts have been excluded except in cases where they are substantial or else the original register from which they were taken has since disappeared. In these cases the word Extracts or the abbreviation Extr. has been used. In spite of all precautions, however, it is more than likely that many extracts have slipped through disguised as complete copies. Difficulty has sometimes arisen in that a copy has in the past sometimes been described as "Extracts" when in fact it gives an accurate summary of every entry as with most copies, or when it contains a complete copy of a restricted number of years. These have been included in the index as ordinary copies.

International Genealogical Index (IGI)

The International Genealogical Index is an index of material contained in the computer of the Genealogical Society of the Church of Latter Day Saints at Utah, U.S.A. Consisting mainly of baptismal entries with a smaller number of marriages, the Index derives its information from three main sources:

a) Entries submitted by members of the Church, arising from their own research.

b)   Entries prior to 1875 extracted from parish registers, bishops transcripts and modern copies of both. Covering dates for extracts are given in the texts for each parish covered.

c)   Other records, such as those of the deceased members of the Church.

Copies of the Index on microfiche are held by the Society of Genealogists, London, the Institute of Heraldic & Genealogical Studies, Canterbury, the libraries of many local Family History Societies and at the Branch Libraries of the Church of Jesus Christ of Latter Day Saints.
The Index is not intended as a data source and should not be used without reference to the original source given. As a guide to name distribution and for locating specific references the Index is valuable. There is however a danger in assuming references give accurate full coverage. In many cases, only extracts are included and many of these together with the full extracts have been consolidated under one name group, often at variance with a correct interpretation.

See also Genealogists Magazine Vol 19 No 5 and Federation News & Digest Vol 1 No 3, Vol 2 No 1 and Vol 3 No 3.

Nonconformist Chapels and Catholic Churches

Urban chapels and churches have been included at the end of the list of Anglican parishes for each town - Catholic churches first and then Nonconformist chapels.

Rural chapels and churches have been listed under the Anglican Parish although in many cases the names of the places in which they were situated were better known than those of the Anglican parishes, or they drew their Congregations from several Anglican parishes. Suitable cross references under the names of these places have been made. In the case of Nonconformist or Catholic churches which were founded before 1837 but which did not surrender registers, the starting date of registers in church hands is noted even if these are after 1837. Copies made at the time of the surrender of the orginal registers have been listed under OR rather than Cop as frequently fresh entries were added to these after 1837.

Whenever the information has been easily accessible an attempt has been made to include every known Nonconformist chapel and Catholic Mission or Church in existence before 1837 whether registers are known or not. In the case of existing Nonconformist Churches, many Church Secretaries failed to return completed questionnaires, and the name and foundation church have been entered with the cryptic phrase "No information". When a "nil return" has been made, the phrase "No registers known" has been used. In the case of pre-1837 Nonconformist chapels now no longer in existence, as with most other information, the thoroughness of the listing varies to some degree from county to county, and whilst it is true that further research would bring to light many unlisted defunct chapels, the time has simply not been available to explore this subject thoroughly. However, all denominational Unions and Associations were approached in an effort to locate any registers.

Roman Catholics

In the case of many Catholic Missions and Churches covering a wide area cross references have been put in for the principal Anglican parishes mentioned in the registers. All Diocesan Archivists and Bishops' Secretaries have been asked if they held any registers.

Independents

This designation has been used throughout except when an existing church is referred to for the location of registers when the more familiar "Congregationalist" (or the abbreviation 'Cong') has been used, e.g. Minister, X Cong. Ch.

Baptists

It is important to bear in mind that the abbreviation 'C' is used here for adult Baptisms. Except in a few counties it has not been possible in the time available to distinguish between General Baptist and Particular Baptist churches, although these were of course entirely separate denominations.

Methodists

An entry has normally been made under the Circuit heading listing known churches within the Circuit in 1837 and any circuit registers and referring readers to any individual church which kept registers. Under the name of the Church, the circuit to which it belonged in 1837 is listed. Sometimes more detail on the administrative history is given.

Society of Friends (Quakers)

An entry has been made for each Monthly Meeting, listing meeting houses within it at various periods and any Monthly Meeting registers. It is then necessary to consult the entries for individual meeting houses to discover if there were additional registers, though when only one or two isolated meeting houses within the Monthly Meeting kept registers these have been indicated. Under the name of each meeting house is the Monthly Meeting to which it belonged at various times, to which reference should be made to discover whether registers exist.

Newspapers

Only newspapers which exist in a fairly consecutive series for a few years or more have been included.

ABBREVIATIONS FOR

NATIONAL RECORD REPOSITORIES AND LIBRARIES

See also the lists at the beginning of the "General Information" section of each county.

BI   Borthwick Institute of Historical Reseach, St. Anthony's Hall, Peaseholme Green, York Y01 2PW. Admission by prior appointment only.

BL   Department of Manuscripts, The British Library, Great Russell Street, London WC1B 3DG. A reader's ticket is necessary.

Bod   Department of Western Manuscripts, Bodleian Library, Oxford OX1 3BG.

C of A   College of Arms, Queen Victoria Street, London E.C.4 The Library is not open to the public.

GL   Guildhall Library, Aldermanbury, London, EC2P 2EJ.

HL   House of Lords Record Office, House of Lords, London SW1A 0AA.

IGI   The Computer File Index of the Genealogical Department of the Church of Jesus Christ of Latter-Day Saints, 50 East North Temple Street, Salt Lake City, Utah 84150, U.S.A.

NLW   National Library of Wales, Aberystwyth, SY23 3BU.

NRA   National Register of Archives, Quality House, Quality Court, Chancery Lane, London WC2A 1HP.

Phil Ms   Manuscript copies of Parish Registers in the possession of Phillimore & Co. Ltd., Shopwyke Hall, Chichester, Sussex PO20 6BQ. A fee is normally charged.

PRO   The Public Record Office, Chancery Lane, London WC2A 1LR. A reader's ticket is necessary.

SG   Society of Genealogists, 37 Harrington Gardens, London SW7 4JX. The library is open to non-members on payment of half-daily and daily fees.

SLC   Genealogical Department of the Church of Jesus Christ of Latter-Day Saints, 50 East North Temple Street, Salt Lake City, Utah 84150, U.S.A.

SRO   Scottish Record Office, P.O. Box 36, H.M. General Register House, Edinburgh EH1 3YY.

URCHS   United Reformed Church History Society, 86 Tavistock Place, London WC1H 9RT. Admission by prior appointment only.

OTHER ABBREVIATIONS USED THROUGHOUT THE SERIES

Add Ms   Additional Manuscript (British Library)

Arch Soc   Archaeological Society

B   Burials

Bapt   Baptist (never Baptisms)

Boyd   Marriage Index compiled by the late Percival Boyd (copies at SG and SLC)

Boyd Misc   In Boyd's Miscellaneous volumes (see NIPR, vol. 1, pp. 201-5)

BT   Bishops Transcript. For convenience this abbreviation has been used for any annual Parish Register copies sent in to an ecclesiastical superior.

c   circa

C   Baptisms (also used for Adult Baptisms of Baptists)

Calv Meth   Calvinistic Methodist (Presbyterian Church of Wales)

Cat   Catalogue(d)

Cath Ch   Roman Catholic Church

Cem   Cemetery

Ch Sec   Church Secretary (for name and address consult current yearbook of the relevant denomination)

CI   Society of Genealogists' Great Card Index

Circ Supt or Circ Sperint
          Circuit Superintendent (for name and address consult current edition of 'Minutes of the Methodist Conference')

cl   closed

Cong   Congregationalist (used only when referring to present name of Church, otherwise Ind is used)

Constit Meetings
          Constituent Meetings

Cop   Modern copies

CRS or Cath RS Catholic Record Society publications

D   Deaths

Dioc   Diocese

disc   discontinued

D Mss	In boxes of Deeds and Manuscripts at the Society of Genealogists
Extr	Extracts
f	founded
Gen Bapt	General Baptist
I	Indexed
Inc	Incumbent. For convenience this has also been used for Catholic Parish Priests
Ind	Independent (Congregationalist)
Lady Hunt Conn	Countess of Huntingdon's Connexion
M	Marriages
Meth NC	Methodist New Connexion
Mf	microfilm
M Lic	Marriage Licences
MM	Monthly Meeting
Ms	Manuscript
NIPR	National Index of Parish Registers
N & Q	Notes and Queries
Nonc	Nonconformist
OR	Original Registers
p/s	photostat
Part Bapt	Particular Baptist
Phil	Phillimore's printed Marriage Series (Number refers to volume number in the appropriate county series)
Phil Ms	See 'National Record Repositories and Libraries' above
PR	Parish Register
Pres	Presbyterian
Prim Meth	Primitive Methodist
Ptd	printed
regs	registers

RC	Roman Catholics
S of F	Society of Friends (Quakers)
Supt	Superintendent
Ts	Typescript
Unit	Unitarian
Vol	Volume
Wes	Wesleyan Methodist
Z	Births
+	Onwards. Invariably means 'until after 1837', and in the case of original registers normally indicates that the registers continue from the date listed up to the present

STAFFORDSHIRE

STAFFORDSHIRE

ACKNOWLEDGEMENTS

Acknowledgement is made for the help given by the staff of the Staffordshire County Record Office, Lichfield Joint Record Office, numerous libraries and many incumbents.

Acknowledgement is also made for the help and guidance given by members of the Birmingham and Midland Society for Genealogy and Heraldry who initiated this work.

STAFFORDSHIRE

GENERAL INFORMATION

INTRODUCTION

Staffordshire is one of the North-West Midland counties. In 1837 it was bounded on the north-west by Cheshire, on the north-east by Derbyshire, was just touched on the east by Leicestershire, had Warwickshire on the south-east, Worcestershire on the south and Shropshire on the west. It was some 55 miles from the north to the south and some 35 miles from west to east.

The area of the County was about 1340 square miles. Through administrative changes made at different periods during the nineteenth century, it gained 1,594 acres from Derbyshire and Warwickshire and gave up 3,969 acres to Worcestershire. In more recent times, a considerable part of the southern industrial part of the County was annexed by the formation of the new County of West Midlands in 1974.

Staffordshire was anciently divided into five Hundreds, named after the meeting places of the Hundred Moots. Totmonslow Hundred was in the north, Pirehill Hundred in the north-west, Offlow Hundred in the east, Cuttlestone Hundred in the west and Seisdon Hundred in the South.

The increase in population of Staffordshire during the nineteenth century was enormous. In 1801 it stood at 242,693, but by 1901 it had increased to 1,234,533. The increase was almost wholly in the industrial districts of the Black Country, the potteries and Burton-on-Trent, as evidenced by the following figures:

	1801	1901
Burton-on-Trent	5,278	43,060
Kingswinford	6,464	38,490
Walsall	10,399	87,464
Wolverhampton	12,565	94,187
The Potteries (Burslem, Stoke-on-Trent and Wolstanton	27,671	238,563

On the other hand, the population of the purely agricultural market towns and villages which lay off the railways increased very little and in some cases declined:

	1801	1901
Abbot's Bromley	1,318	1,318
Draycott-in-the-Moors	491	351
Eccleshall	3,734	4,186
Enville	799	645
Gnosall	2,246	2,085

Thus, by the early to middle nineteenth century, many additional parishes began to be created in the industrial towns. There was also strong support for nonconformity, particulary Methodism. Methodist chapels listed for Staffordshire outnumbered all the other nonconformist denominations by over 75%. In particular, Primitive Methodism had its origins in the County.

RECORD REPOSITORIES

SRO   **Staffordshire Record Office**, County Buildings, Eastgate Street, Stafford, ST16 2LZ. Telephone: Stafford 3121 Extension 7910. Hours: Monday to Thursday 9.00am - 1.00pm, 2.00pm - 5.00pm; Friday 9.00am - 1.00pm, 2.00pm to 4.30pm. (Closed Saturdays, Sundays, Bank Holidays and the Tuesday following Bank Holidays). For readers who are unable to visit the Record Office during the week, a limited Saturday service is operated in conjunction with the William Salt Library. Up to six items from the County Record Office may be transferred to the William Salt Library for use on a Saturday, but only five readers may book for each Saturday. Documents should be ordered as early as possible, but at the latest by 3.00pm on the preceeding Friday. The Record Office holds many of the records of the County and is the repository for most of the original Parish Registers, particularly for the northern and central parts of the County. A list of Staffordshire Parish Registers and copies and a list of deposited nonconformist registers is available for a small charge. The Record Office has a wide selection of Census returns on microfilm, excluding Stoke-on-Trent and some South Staffordshire districts, for 1841, 1851, 1861 and 1871. Many maps are available for the Conty and a handlist has been published as a guide to early manuscript estate maps relating to the County which are to be found in the County Record Offices or other repositories. There is also a reader's guide available for consultation containing lists of specialised data sources for such topics as railways, canals and topography.

LJRO   **LICHFIELD JOINT RECORD OFFICE**, Bird Street, Lichfield. Telephone: Lichfield 56787. Hours: Monday, Tuesday, Thursday and Friday 10.00am - 5.15pm; Wednesday 10.00am - 4.45pm. This is the main repository for the records of the Diocese of Lichfield. The Diocese covered, not only Staffordshire, but also parts of Derbyshire, Shropshire and Warwickshire. It holds the original Bishop's Transcripts, Marriage Allegations and Bonds and Wills. A guide to the Diocesan Probate and Church Commissioners' records has been published (see reference list).

WSL   **WILLIAM SALT LIBRARY**, Eastgate Street, Stafford. Telephone: Stafford 52276. Hours: Tuesday, Wednesday, Thursday 9.30am - 12.45pm, 1.45pm - 5.00pm; Friday 9.30am - 12.45pm, 1.45pm - 5.00pm; Saturday 9.30am - 1.00pm. The library, adjacent to the County Record Office, holds an extensive collection of works relating to local history. This includes copies of the printed parish registers, together with a large collection of manuscript transcripts of parish registers and a collection of local newspapers.

DR **DIOCESAN REGISTRY**, 20 St John Street, Lichfield, WS13 6PB. Telephone: Lichfield 2060 and 2491. The Diocesan Registry holds a complete set of microfilms of all Staffordshire Bishop's Transcripts which may be hired if required.

DA **DIOCESAN ARCHIVES**, Archdiocese of Birmingham, Cathedral House, St Chad's Queensway, Birmingham, West Midlands B4 6EU. This holds the archives of the Roman Catholic Archdiocese of Birmingham, which includes a number of Staffordshire registers, both originals and copies. The archives may be consulted, but because of limitation on space it is necessary to book in advance.

ChRO **CHESHIRE RECORD OFFICE**, The Castle, Chester, CH1 2DN. Telephone: Chester 602574. This holds the records of the Cheshire and Staffordshire Quarterly Meetings of the Society of Friends. A few Staffordshire wills are also held, but these usually refer to limited powers granted in respect of interests in the Archdeaconry of Chester and should, therefore, be duplicated at Lichfield and at the PCC.

WRO **WORCESTERSHIRE RECORD OFFICE**, Shirehall, Worcester WR1 1TR, also at St Helen's, Fish Street, Worcester WR1 2HN. Telephone: Worcester 23400. Hours: Monday to Friday 9.15am - 4.45pm. The Bishop's Transcripts and Probate records for a few South Staffordshire parishes are held at the St Helen's office.

BRL **BIRMINGHAM REFERENCE LIBRARY**, Paradise Circus, Queensway, Birmingham. Telephone: 021-235-4219 (History Dept, 4th Floor 021-235-4549; Local Studies, 6th floor 021-235-4220). Hours: Monday and Friday 9.00am - 6.00pm; Tuesday, Wednesday and Thursday 9.00am - 8.00pm; Saturday 9.00am - 5.00pm. This holds many printed parish registers, directories, newspapers, etc, particularly for the southern parts of Staffordshire.

BOT-PL **BURTON LIBRARY**, Roverside, High Street, Burton-on-Trent DE14 1AH. Telephone: Burton-on-Trent 43271. Hours: Monday, Tuesday, Thursday and Friday 9.30am - 6.00pm; Wednesday 9.30am - 1.00pm; Saturday 9.15am - 1.00pm. This library holds deposits of a number of Wesleyan, Primitive and United Methodist registers, most of which are post-1837. One Independent register for the High Street Chapel commencing in 1808 is probably a copy of the original made prior to its surrender to the Register General.

DPL **DUDLEY LIBRARY**, 3 St James' Road, Dudley, West Midlands DY1 1HU. Telephone: Dudley 55433 (after 5.00pm and Saturdays, 56321). Hours: Main Library, Monday to Friday 9.00am - 7.00pm; Saturday 9.00am - 5.00pm; Archives/Local History Search Room, Monday, Wednesday and Friday 9.00am - 1.00pm, 2.00pm - 5.00pm, Tuesday and Thursday 2.00pm - 7.00pm. When the Local History Search Room is closed, material may be made available in the main library by prior arrangement. It is recommended that advance notice of a visit to the Search Room should be given. The Archives Department of the Library is a recognised repository under the Parochial Registers and Records Measure Act of 1978 for records in the

Deanery of Dudley (Diocese of Worcester) and the Deanery of Himley (Diocese of Lichfield). Staffordshire parish registers deposited are Kingswingford, Wordsley, Lower Gornal, Upper Gornal and Quarry Bank. The Local History Collection contains material relating to the area of the present Metropolitan Borough and the surrounding areas of the Black Country and covers a wide range of local topics. The holdings include microfilmed copies of newspapers, microfilms of the 1841 to 1871 Census Returns for the area of the present Metropolitan Borough and Directories.

HPL **HANLEY LIBRARY,** City Central Library, Bethesda Street, Hanley, Stoke-on-Trent ST1 3RS. Telephone: Stoke-on-Trent 25108 and 26356. Hours: Monday, Tuesday, Wednesday and Friday 9.00am - 8.00pm; Thursday 9.00am - 5.00pm; Saturday 9.00am - 1.00pm. This library holds a considerable number of transcripts and microfilms for local parishes, including some records for nonconformist chapels.

NPL **NEWCASTLE LIBRARY,** Ironmarket, Newcastle, Staffs, ST5 1AT. Telephone: Newcastle 618125. Hours: Monday, Wednesday and Friday 9.00am - 7.00pm; Tuesday and Thursday 9.00am - 5.00pm; Saturday 9.00am - 1.00pm. This holds a number of original Methodist registers, one of which for the Ebenezer Chapel starts in 1812 and was not surrendered to the Registrar General. The library also holds a number of microfilm copies and transcripts for local parishes, together with deposited local nonconformist material. Many other items held include Census Returns, Rate Books, Directories, Hearth Tax and Newspapers. A booklet covering these holdings has been published.

SDL **SMETHWICK DISTRICT LIBRARY,** High Street, Smethwick, Warley, West Midlands. Telephone: 021-558-0497. This holds a number of original parish registers. Only those for Rowley Regis begin prior to 1837 and many of these were damaged in a fire at the church in 1913 and are not generally available to the public. A few nonconformist registers, all post 1837 are also held.

WaPL **WALSALL LIBRARY,** Archives Service, Central Library, Lichfield Street, Walsall WS1 1TR, West Midlands. Telephone: Walsall 21244 ext 3111. Hours: Monday to Friday 9.30am - 7.00pm; Saturday 9.30am - 5.00pm. This holds a number of original Methodist registers, the earliest commencing in 1838, and microfilm copies of local Non-Parochial registers deposited in the PRO.

WoPL **WOLVERHAMPTON LIBRARY,** Central Library, Snow Hill, Wolverhampton WV1 3AX. Telephone: Wolverhampton 773824. Hours: Monday to Friday 10.00am - 7.00pm; Saturday 9.30am - 5.00pm. This library has a large collection of original Methodist registers. One of these for Darlington Street commences in 1793 and is presumed to be a copy of the surrendered register. Transcripts for a number of local parishes are also held.

OTHER ABBREVIATIONS USED

CMI	Coker Marriage Index
Confms	Confirmations
Derbys	Derbyshire.
Erec	Erected
Ex par	Ex parochial
GBMI	Great Birmingham Marriage Index
Ind Calv	Independent Calvinist
L	Diocese of Lichfield
Lic	Licenced (for religious purposes)
Mar I	Marriage Index
MI	Monumental Inscriptions
QM	Quarterly Meeting (S of F)
Reg	Registered as a Dissenting Chapel
Salop	Shropshire
SMI	Staffordshire Marraige Index
W	Diocese of Worcester
Warcs	Warwickshire
Wes Meth Assoc	Wesleyan Methodist Association
Worcs	Worcestershire

Ancient Parishes

There were 183 ancient parishes in Staffordshire of which three were in the town of Stafford and four in the City of Lichfield. Ecclesiastically, the County was mostly in the Archdeaconry of Stafford, Diocese of Lichfield, Province of Canterbury. A few southern parishes were in the Diocese of Worcester and, since 1905 when the Diocese of Birmingham was created, several parishes near to Birmingham have been in that Diocese. A number of parishes have been transferred to other counties since 1837. Excluding the county boundary changes made in 1974, these were Upper Arley, Broome and Clent to Worcestershire, Handsworth and Harborne to Warwickshire and Sheriff Hales to Shropshire. Against these losses the County gained Croxall and Stappenhill from Derbyshire and Wilnecote from Warwickshire. Some parishes served villages and/or hamlets in two counties. These were:- Bobbington, part Staffordshire, part Shropshire; Clifton Campville, part Staffordshire, part Chilcote Chapelry formerly in Derbyshire, but later Leicestershire; Tamworth, part Staffordshrie, part Warwickshire of which some parts were transferred to Staffordshire in 1842; and Woore, originally in the parish of Mucklestone, Staffordshire, but now in Shropshire.

Because of these complications, it has not been possible to obtain perfect consistency with the other volumes in this series. Therefore, in this volume, all parishes which have been or are located in Staffordshire or which have served Staffordhsire villages have been included. This will, on occasions, result in a parish occuring under two diffferent counties in this series.

For reasons of historical comparison the population of each parish (including that of all its chapelries) in 1831 is given after the parish dedication.

ECCLESIASTICAL DIVISIONS

From 1228 until the dissolution of the Cathedral Priory of Coventry in 1539, both the secular collegiate church of Lichfield and the Benedictine priory church of Coventry were Cathedrals for a Diocese, stretching from the Ribble in Lancashire to Edgehill in south-east Warwickshire. In 1541, the Archdeaconry of Chester (Cheshire, South Lancashire and parts of Flint and Denbeigh) became part of the newly-created See of Chester. From then until 1836 the Diocese covered Staffordshire, Derbyshire, Northern Shropshire and Northern and Eastern Warwickshire. It was called "Coventry and Lichfield" until the mid-seventeenth century and then "Lichfield and Coventry" until 1836. The Archdeaconry of Birmingham covering virtually the whole of Warwickshire was transferred to the Diocese of Worcester in 1836 although, for a time, the ecclesiastical courts of Lichfield continued to exercise jurisdiction. In 1905 this Archdeaconry, together with parts of Staffordshire which included Upper Arley, became the Diocese of Birmingham. Throughout the period Clent and Broome, a detached island of Staffordshire in Worcestershire, and also Rowley Regis were in the Diocese of Worcester. On the Shropshire border, Bobbington was transferred to the Diocese of Hereford on the abolition of Peculiar jurisdiction.

ORIGINAL PARISH REGISTERS

A total of 228 churches and chapels have been listed which were in existence prior to 1837 as places of worship for the Established Church. Each of these is listed under its own place name, although in the case of a chapelry this has been cross-referenced to the parent church. Approximately two-thirds of the County's parish registers have been deposited in the County Record Office and it is expected that many more will follow as a result of the Parochial Registers and Records Measures Act of 1978. Thus, these listings will soon be outdated, but usually as a result of further deposits from incumbents. A few registers have been deposited at other approved locations. Dudley Library has the registers of Gornal, Kingswinford and Wordsley; Lichfield Joint Record Office has the registers of St Chad, St Mary and St Michael and all of Lichfield; Sandwell Library has the registers of Rowley Regis and West Bromwich.

Of the registers for Staffordshire, fourteen commence in 1538, two in 1539, three in the 1540's and twenty-three in the 1550's. The registers of St Martin, Tipton appear to commence in 1513 which, if true, would make them amongst the earliest known registers in the country. However, there may be a more logical explanation. Whilst purporting to commence in 1513, the entries for 1518 are followed by an entry for 1579. This suggests that, as the early part of the register was merely a transcript of the original, the correct commencing date should be 1573 and not 1513. This conclusion is confirmed by family reconstructions covering this period in the register.

The ravages of time have taken their toll on Staffordshire registers. A number for St Giles, Rowley Regis were either badly damaged or burned in a church fire on 18th June 1913. Although in an iron chest, water damage and charring caused some of them to shrink to half their size. The register from 1684 to 1714 was "soaked with water that, in spite of all efforts to preserve it, it rotted away and had to be destroyed". Burial registers from 1760 to 1812 were, at the time of the fire, being transcribed away from the church and were thereby saved. Fortunately, the Staffordshire Parish Register Society has published its transcript to 1812, serving as a constant reminder of the value of transcribing original registers. What remains of the registers is preserved at Smethwick District Library, but many are illegible. However, some have been photocopied. A few other records have been similarly preserved. William Kelsall, an antiquarian from Batterley, transcribed the registers of Audley, Betley, Burslem, Keele, Madeley and Norton-on-the-Moors at the start of the eighteenth century. Two of these parishes appear to have lost their earliest registers since the transcription. Burslem, commencing in 1637, compares with Kelsall's transcript commencing in 1578; and Madeley, commencing in 1678, compares with Kelsall's transcript commencing in 1567. Both of these registers have now been printed by the Staffordshire Parish Register Society. Unfortunately, other parishes have not been so lucky. In the 1831 survey of registers, those for Bushbury were given a commencement date of 1747 with the comment that the earlier registers had been destroyed. Also, the baptismal registers for St John the Baptist, Hanley from 1803 to 1842 are thought to have been destroyed during the Chartist riots of 1842.

The registers of Kingswinford often lead to confusion. Those for the parish church of St Mary's commence in 1603. By 1831 the parish had expanded to such an extent that a new church, that of Holy Trinity, was erected. Although in the village of Wordsley, and being approximately one mile from St Mary's, the new church assumed the role of the Parish Church of Kingswinford. St Mary's registers were transferred to Holy Trinity where the entries were continued. St Mary's then became a chapel of ease and commenced new registers. It became a parish church again in its own right in 1846. The consequence of the transfer of these early registers is that the registers of Holy Trinity, Wordsley are often given as commencing in 1603 and those for Kingswinford in 1832.

BISHOP'S TRANSCRIPTS

Unless indicated otherwise, all Bishop's Transcripts are held at the Lichfield Joint Record Office.

Diocese of Lichfield. The Bishop's Transcripts were, until 1968 held at the Diocesan Registry, Lichfield, but were transferred to the present Lichfield Joint Record Office on the provision of a document storage room. Dates and gaps recorded here are based on a detailed listing held at the Lichfeild Joint Record Office. This was prepared at the time of the transfer of the transcripts from the Diocesan Registry, but has since been updated for a number of parishes, which have been systematically rechecked.
The Diocesan Visitation was usually made every three years, register transcripts then being returned, unlike the normal practice of sending retuns annually. Consequently, many of the transcripts are bulky. For the larger industrial parishes three years of baptisms, marriages and burials could cover up to a dozen skins each about three feet square. Register transcripts usually commence in 1660, although a few parishes commence a few years earlier. There are a few exceptions to this, for example, Brewood (1618 only) and Armitage (1623-26), but there are no continuous runs before 1653 (Shenstone). The transcripts are reasonably complete after 1700 and incumbents in the 1690's appear to have been encouraged to fill up post-1660 gaps. There are two series: the pre-1813 irregular shaped parchment sheets in bundles, usually one per parish, but more in the case of populous parishes; and the post 1813 series on printed forms. After 1837 parishes began to stop sending returns though some parishes, Lichfield Cathedral, Lichfield St Chad and Stone continued to 1892, Stetton to 1893 and Shenstone to 1910.

Transcripts for several parishes appeared in Terriers and these are also deposited at the Lichfield Joint Record Office. Generally, these were for short periods and include Blore-Ray (1677-79), Blymhill (1762-66, 1770-73) and Burslem St John. (1744-47).

Diocese of Worcester. These transcripts are at Worcester Record Office and include three Staffordshire parishes, Broome (1613), Clent (1612) and Rowley Regis (1606), all of which start much earlier than other Staffordshire parishes. The pre-1701 transcripts are in parish order, but post-1701 transcripts are arranged by year and then by Deanery.

Peculiars. All the transcripts which have survived for the Peculiars, with the exception of Bobbington, are at the Lichfield Joint Record Office. In the case of Bobbington, the pre-1812 transcripts are at the British Library, whilst post-1812 transcripts are at the Lichfield Joint Record Office.

MODERN COPIES

As far as possible, all known copies, whether printed, typescript, manuscript photocopy or microfilm which are in record repositories or libraries in the United Kingdom have been included. However, where a copy covers exactly the same period as the printed volume (often being the source material), only the printed volume is given. No reference is made for material outside the United Kingdom, such as the vast holdings of the Genealogical Society of the Church of Jesus Christ of Latter Day Saints, although these have been given in previous volumes in this series.

Every attempt has been made to obtain the latest position on typescript and manuscript copies, but the frequency of register transcribing continually changes the position. In a number of cases, modern copies of the same register have been desposited in several places. For example, there is a manuscript copy for St Luke's of Cannock in the William Salt Library, an index with the Birmingham and Midland Society for Genealogy and Heraldry and microfilm copies of a manuscript at the Central Library, Hanley and at Newcastle Library. Where multiple copies exist, dates given for the coverage of each copy vary and it is suspected that in some cases these dates are not as precise as one would hope. However, to verify the dates in every copy accurately has been, regretfully, beyond the resources available.

PRINTED COPIES

The Staffordshire Parish Register Society was founded at the turn of the century and at first several registers were published each year. Following the onset of the first World War, the rate of publication dropped to one each year and after 1940, to one every two years. Since then, the increasing costs of hard-back publications has resulted in the Society's most recent publication, of the registers of Wednesfield in conjunction with the Birmingham Society for Genealogy and Heraldry, appearing in paper-back. Registers for fifty-six chrches have been published in a total of some eighty volumes. In addition, a further volume covers the Roman Catholic registers of Chillington, Cresswell, Walsall and Wolverhampton. In general, most volumes do not continue beyond 1812.

Staffordshire is one of the Midland counties covered by the Birmingham and Midland Society for Genealogy and Heraldry. Amongst the Society's numerous publications over the past few years are six Staffordshire registers, namely, Adbaston, Audley, Church Eaton, Hanley, High Offley and Madeley, as well as the joint publication with the Staffordshire Parish Register Society. Another seven Staffordshire volumes are currently in stages of transciption or publication.

A number of Staffordshire registers have been printed by other bodies. Willmore published Rushall and Walsall, the Burton-on-Trent Archaeological Society published St Modwen for the period 1538 to 1610 and the Staffordshire Catholic Historical Society published confirmation lists for the County from 1768 to 1816. In addition, registers from two parishes inlcluded in this volume, but which have been affected by county boundary changes, have also been printed. The registers for Upper Arley have been pubished by the Worcestershire Parish Register Society and those for Sheriff Hales by the Shropshire Parish Register Society.

TYPESCRIPT AND MANUSCRIPT COPIES

The William Salt Library holds an extensive number of typescript and manuscript copies of parish registers. Many of these were transcribed under the auspices of the Staffordshire Parish Register Society. The Society of Genealogists holds a number of typescript and manuscript copies of registers.

A number of the larger libraries in the County hold typescript and manuscript copies for local parishes. The Birmingham and Midland Society for Genealogy and Heraldry holds a number of manuscript and typescript copies, either deposited by their members or as a result of their own transcriptions.

MICROFILM COPIES

A number of parish registers have been microfilmed mainly for retention in a local library. In addition, most of the nonconformist registers deposited at the Public Record Office have been microfilmed. Copies are usually deposited at the County Record Office and in the main local library. There is a complete set of microfilms of all Bishop's Transcripts for the Diocese of Lichfield (the originals being at the Lichfield Joint Record Office). The microfilms are held at the Diocesan Registry, 20 St John Street, Lichfield, WS13 6PD, from where they can be hired by individuals at a charge (1981) of £6.90 for one reel, £8.05 for two reels, £9.20 for three reels, etc.

MARRIAGE INDEXES

There are five marriage indexes which cover some of the parishes included in the Staffordshire volume. The aim of the General Staffordshire Marriage Index is to cover the whole County. The Greater Birmingham Marriage Index is included because a number of South Staffordshire parishes, for example Handsworth, will appear in this index. The last three indexes are unlikely to be extended, but are given for completeness.

The Staffordshire Marriage Index is a slip index currently in the process of compilation by members of the Birmingham and Midland Society for Genealogy and Heraldry. The aim is to include all marraiges for the County up to 1837 regardless of whether or not they appear in other indexes. It is hoped this will be eventually published in some form by the Society. By June 1981, fifty-eight parishes had been included, although not necesarily for the whole period to 1837. Over twenty additional parishes are currently being indexed so that increase in coverage is likely to be rapid. Enquiries for a specific entry, but not total name coverage, should be made to Mrs J Dunn, 1 Common Walk, Huntington, Cannock, Staffs, together with a stamped addressed envelope and a small donation towards the maintenance of the index. Where unsuccessful, the enquirer's reference slip will be inserted in the index.

The Greater Birmingham Index is also being compiled by members of the same Society. A number of the northern parishes originally in Staffordshire but now part of Greater Birmingham, such as Great Barr, Harborne, Handsworth and Smethwick are likely to be included in both this and the Staffordshire Marriage Index. Initially, the team of indexers are concentrating on the period from 1801 to 1837. Staffordshire parishes so far included are Handsworth and Harborne. Enquiries, enclosing a stamped addressed envelope should be sent to Mr F.V. Winchurch, 3 Dunns Coppice, Ledbury, Herefordshire, HR8 2HR.

Coker's Staffordshire Index was compiled by the late John Coker from the parish registers printed by the Staffordshire Parish Register Society. With the exception of Gnossall and Wolverhampton, it covers all printed volumes to the end of 1973. The index is for males only and is in typescript form. Copies of the index are held by the Lichfield Joint Record Office and the Birmingham and Midland Society for Genealogy and Heraldry.

Coker's Wolverhampton Marriage Index, also compiled by the late John Coker, was taken from the Wolverhampton printed registers from 1661 to 1837. The Index is typescript with copies held by the Lichfield Joint Record Office and the Birmingham and Midland Society for Genealogy and Heraldry.

Boyd's Marriage Index has no section for Staffordshire, but marriages from four parishes, Aldridge, Bobbington, Marchington and Rowley Regis are included in the Boyd's Miscellaneous Volumes. The periods covered vary from 15 years for Marchington to 160 years for Bobbington. In all, less than 1% of the County is thereby covered.

MARRIAGE BONDS AND ALLEGATIONS

Marriage bonds and allegations for the area covered by the jurisdiction of the Diocese of Lichfield are held at the Lichfield Joint Record Office. There are only a few bonds extant prior to 1660. From 1660 to 1670, whilst there are a number of bonds, these are probably not complete. After 1670 nearly all the bonds sworn are believed extant. Those prior to 1660 form one small bundle with yearly bundles thereafter. Within each year, the bonds are sorted by initial letter of the groom's name, but no further and there may be some mis-sorts. There are a number of manuscript indexes covering the period to 1713, but no indexes exist for later years.

Bonds and allegations sworn in respect of licences issued by the Lichfield Peculiar Courts are not included with the Diocesan bonds, but kept separate. Indexes exist for only a few of the Peculiars and then only for part of the period covered.

The original bonds, affidavits and allegations covered by the jurisdiction of the Diocese of Worcester, of which there are some 134,000, are kept at the Worcestershire Record Office. These marriage bonds and allegations have been microfilmed by the Church of Jesus Christ of Latter Day Saints and copies are held at Salt Lake City.

ROMAN CATHOLICS AND NONCONFORMISTS

Nonconformity in Staffordshire has always had many followers. Some measure of their support can be obtained from returns made under the 1851 Census of Religious Establishments. All churches and chapels were required to give information about the churches including their Sunday services attendances on 30th March 1851. The County population was then 608,716 and the returns for Sunday service attendances showed that 129,962 attended in the morning; 83,404 in the afternoon; and 83,881 in the evening. Of these, those attending protestant nonconformist services were 54,918 in the morning; 36,266 in the afternoon; and 52,917 in the evening. These figures indicate that almost 50% of all attendances were in nonconformist chapels. This does not mean that a similar percentage of baptisms, marriages and burials would be registered in nonconformist chapels, as undoubtedly the larger proportion of people still had these events solemnised within the Established Church.

Roman Catholic churches and nonconformist chapels founded before 1837 and given here have been compiled from many sources. However, for the most part, they will have occured in one or more of the following three sources:

i) from the 1851 religious census returns. These give the name and address of the place of worship, the size and attendance for these churches and chapels and a date for their erection. Only those founded or erected before 1838 have been included. A copy of thse returns on microfilm are held in the County Record Office.

ii) from returns of registration of nonconformist chapels and meeting houses required by the Toleration Act of 1689. A compilation of these returns by B Donaldson entitled "The Registration of Dissenting Chapels and Meeting Houses in Staffordshire 1689-1852" was published by the Staffordshire Record Society in 1960.

iii) from county directories and, in particular, White's "History, Gazeteer and Directory of Staffordhsire" published in 1834 and in 1851.

With the exception of the Society of Friends, only places described as "church" or "chapel", as opposed to "meeting place", "room" etc, have been included. A considerable number of chapels so listed no longer exist and for many there appear to be no records extant. No doubt, further research would bring to light registers for a few of these chapels, but it was considered better to publish what is known, rather than wait for a life-long research project and publish nothing. Many chapels, therefore, are listed where little is known beyond their foundation date and location. However, it is hoped that even this may be helpful in guiding researches into which denominations were active in a particular area.

Anglican churches have been listed under their parish name and Anglican chapelries under their local name, cross-referenced to the parent parish. In the case of Roman Catholic and nonconformist chapels, these have been listed either after the Anglican parish church or chapelry. Again, cross-referencing has been made. For the majority of nonconformist chapels, a date of origin has been given. This is usually either the date claimed for its foundation, the date registered, or the date of erection. Only one of these dates is given and this is usually the earliest date identified.

ROMAN CATHOLICS

Staffordshire has a relatively large number of pre-1838 churches, 33 being listed here. Those with the earliest origins were usually attached to the country houses of Catholic gentry, such as the Giffard family at Blackladies and Long Birch (Brewood) and the FitzHerberts at Swynnerton, or to the Catholic seminaries or schools, Oscott (Handsworth) and Sedgley Park. Later, Catholic chapels tended to be in urban areas. This is exemplified by the Registrations of Dissenting Chapels and Meeting Houses. Following the passing of the Second Catholic Relief Act in 1791, thirteen chapels were registered for worship. Of these, only three, Cobridge in Burslem, Stafford and Wolverhampton, were in urban areas whereas later registrations were predominately for chapels in the larger towns.

In total, there are ten registers from the eighteenth century. By far the earliest is that for Chillington, Brewood where there are baptismal registers for 1720-37 and 1762-95, together with a marriage register for 1721-31. The next earliest baptismal register is for Moseley Old Hall, Bushbury commencing in 1773. Other early registers are Cresswell (1780), Lichfield (1788), Tixall (1791), Wolverhampton (1791) but with fragmentary notes from 1754, Oscott (1794), Sedgley (1795), Cobridge (1797) and Yoxall (1797).

Most registers are still located at the churches, although a number of the originals are held in the Diocesan Archives in Birmingham. These archives also hold manuscript copies of other registers as well as a Confirmation Register of Vicars Apostolic 1768-1816 covering the whole of the Midland district. The Staffordshire Parish Register Society has published the Catholic registers of Chillington, Cresswell, Walsall and Wolverhampton.

The Walsall registers of baptisms 1762-66 were taken from a notebook of Pierce Parry, the Priest, and are for a total of 17 baptisms. Further entries of Chillington baptisms have been published by the Staffordshire Catholic Historical Society.

SOCIETY OF FRIENDS

From 1672 to 1783 the Staffordshire Quarterly Meeting covered the Leek Monthly Meeting (1705-83) and the Stafford Monthly Meeting (1713-83). In 1783, the Staffordshire Quarterly Meeting merged with the Cheshire Quarterly Meeting to form the Cheshire and Staffordshire Quarterly Meeting. At the same time, the Leek and Stafford Monthly Meetings also united. The Minute Books for the Staffordshire Quarterly Meetings are deposited at the Staffordshire County Record Office and cover the periods 1672 to 1783 and 1784 to 1800, the latter period probably referring to the records of the Stafford and Leek Monthly Meeting. The registers for the Cheshire and Staffordshire Quarterly Meeting were surrendered to the PRO and date from 1783 for births, 1768 for marriages and 1783 for burials. The digests of submissions to the Registrar General are held at the Cheshire County Record Office. One series, 1688-1837 is mainly devoted to Staffordshire entries, but a further series 1647-1837 also contains some Staffordshire entries.

A considerable number of items relating to the Stafford and to the Stafford and Leek Monthly Meetings are deposited at the Staffordshire County Record Office. These include Records of Suffering, Disownments, Burial notes, etc... some dating back to 1679. There are also holdings of similar documents for the Leek Monthly Meeting, dating back to 1655. The PRO holds the registers for the Uttoxeter Monthly Meeting from 1649 to 1837. The Staffordshire County Record Office also has a number of Minute Books for the Uttoxeter Preparative Meetings commencing 1782.

The Warwickshire Quarterly Meeting was established in 1668, but in 1790 was united to the Leicester Quarterly Meeting to form the Warwick, Leicester and Rutland Quarterly Meeting. Two Staffordshire constituant meetings were included; Tamworth, in the Wishaw (afterwards Baddesley) Monthly Meeting from 1668 to 1710 and in the Birmingham Monthly Meeting (afterwards Warwickshire Monthly Meeting) from 1710 to 1852 and Lichfield in the Birmingham Monthly Meeting from 1816 to 1829. Registers for these Quarterly Meetings and for the Wishaw Monthly Meetings are held at the PRO. Registers for the Birmingham Monthly Meetings are at the Friends Meeting House, Bull Street, Birmingham. Digests for all registers surrendered are also in the Society of Friends Library, Euston Road, London.

Works of reference: Victoria County History of the County of Staffordshire III, page 116 et seq.

BAPTISTS

In total, 29 Baptist chapels have been identified with origins prior to 1838. The main support for the denomination appears to have been in the industrial areas, particularly in the southern part of the County. Of these 29, no fewer than 19 are associated with the industrial towns a few miles from the southern border of the County. Few Baptist chapels, however, registered as Dissenting Places of Worship. The earliest chapel appears to be Brierley Hill, founded about 1776, although there is an indication that an old burial ground at Rushton Spencer in use from 1672 to 1780 may have either belonged to or have been used by the Baptists. Other Baptist chapels founded in the eighteenth century are Coseley Darkhouse (1786), Temple Street Wolverhampton (1785), Willenhall (1787), Hanley (1789), Burton-on-Trent (1790), Burslem (1791), Tamworth (1794), Bilston (1798) and Stafford.

A total of nine chapels surrendered registers, four of which, Darkhouse Chapel Coseley, Brierley Hill, Burton-on-Trent and Coppia Sedgley, commenced in the eighteenth century. No other pre-1838 registers are known.

Works of reference: "Midland Associations" William Stokes 1855, and "History of Baptists" Ivimey, 4 volumes 1811-30.

INDEPENDENTS (CONGREGATIONALISTS)

A total of sixty chapels have been listed, three of which, Burton-on-Trent (1662), Longdon (1672) and Ebenezer Chapel, West Bromwich (1662), were founded in the seventeenth century. A further 19 chapels were founded in the eighteenth century, all with the exception of Wednesbury (1720) in the latter half of the century. Barbara Donaldson, in her compilation of Registrations of Dissenting Chapels (Historical Collections of Staffordshire, Fourth series Volume III), concluded that the spread of the Independent movement in Staffordshire in the nineteenth century took place from a number of centres. She instances Rugeley, where worshipping in the house of a Mrs Sleigh commenced in 1806. The first Independent Minister, Andrew Shawyer, was received in 1810 and a chapel was built in 1813. From 1810 to 1816 Shawyer had established meeting places in six neighbouring villages, although chapels were not built in all these villages.

Registers from thirty-one chapels were surrendered in 1837. It is interesting to note that of the twenty-two chapels with origins before the nineteenth century, all but three surrendered whilst only twelve of the thirty-eight chapels founded in the nineteenth century surrendered. The earliest register is for Temple Street Wolverhampton commencing in 1771. No registers other than those surrendered have been located. However, if the movement did spread out from centres, some of the registers may have covered more than one chapel.

Works of reference: "Congregational Churches in Staffordshire" A G Matthews, Congregational Union 1924; "Nonconformity in Staffordshire 1660-1670" A G Matthews, Congregational Society Transactions Volume 7; "Some Notes on Staffordshire Nonconformity" A G Matthews, Congregational Society Tracts, Volume 12; "Longdon and Lichfield" A J Stevens, Congregational Society Tracts, Volume 3.

PRESBYTERIANS AND UNITARIANS

Thirteen chapels with origins prior to 1838 have been included, classed either as Presbytarian or Unitarian. In a number of cases, the precise denomination is difficult to ascribe since the chapels seem to class themselves as both denominations at different times. Six chapels had their origins in the seventeenth century, Coseley (1662), Newcastle-under-Lyme (1690), Stafford (1687), Uttoxeter (1695), John Street, Wolverhampton (1692) and Walsall (1692), whilst three others, Pensnett Chase Kingswinford (1704), Stone (1705) and Snow Hill Wolverhampton (1700) were in the eighteenth century. With the exception of Tamworth (1724), all the other chapels appear to have been founded in the nineteenth century.

By 1837, four of these chapels had closed, Newcastle-under-Lyme Presbyterian in 1804 (although it reopened after a break as a Unitarian chapel), Shelton in 1831, Stafford about 1810 and Stone in 1808. The Snow Hill chapel in Wolverhampton joined the Trinity Chapel Independents, whilst the Pensnett Chase chapel in Kingswinford crossed the border into Worcestershire around 1796, forming the Park Lane Presbyterian Chapel, Cradley. Of the remaining 7 chapels, 5 surrendered registers, the earliest, Tamworth, commencing 1695. It should be noted that the surrendered registers for the Park Lane Presbyterian chapel at Cradley, listed under Worcestershire, includes one volume covering the period when the chapel was in Staffordshire.

Works of reference: "Congregational Churches in Staffordshire" A G Matthews, Congregational Union 1924.

LADY HUNTINGDON'S CONNEXION

The Connexion was fairly active in the County. Six chapels are listed, of which five were in the southern part of the County, although services were held at many more places. In 1782 services were conducted in Wolverhampton, whilst a chapel existed in Handsworth for a period of 15 years after 1789. A chapel opened at Walsall in 1763 had several Connexional Ministers. In West Bromwich a chapel registered itself under the Dissenting Places of Worship Act in 1751 and this was the only chapel within the Connexion registering in the County. A new chapel was erected in 1785, but the congregation moved to Messenger Street in 1787. This Society became an Independent Congregation in 1800 and it is likely that its surrendered register commencing in 1787 relates to its period within the Connexion. Other chapels erected at Gornal (1777) and Hanley (1784), both of which later became Independent surrendered registers commencing in 1778 and 1786 respectively.

Works of reference: "Victoria County History of the County of Staffordshire" Volume III page 116 et seq.

METHODISTS

Methodism was very strong in Staffordshire and well over 200 chapels have been identified with pre-1838 origins. This number was due partly to the strength of the two major divisions within the movement which resulted in the formation of the Methodist New Connexion and the Primitive Methodist Connexion. The former occured in 1797 over disagreements on organisation and the relationship to the Church of England. It found considerable support in Hanley, especially with the Ridgway family of Cauldon Hall, Shelton who were pottery manufacturers. They, and other prominent inhabitants of Hanley were instrumental in establishing New Connexion chapels and meeting houses throughout the Potteries. Although particularly strong in North Staffordshire, the New Connexion spread into many parts of the county both to rural and to industrial areas. The Primitive Methodist Connexion separated from the parent movement due to the Primitive's fervent manner of preaching and the holding of all-day open-air prayer meetings and its foundations were deeply rooted in this County. Hugh Bourne, born in Stoke-on-Trent, joined the Wesleyan Methodists in 1799 and soon became a local preacher. In 1802 he built a chapel at Harriseahead, chiefly at his own expense. Imitating the revivalist 'Camp Meetings' held in America, with his brother James, William Clowes and others, he held held a Camp Meeting at Mow Cop on the 31st May 1807. The

Wesleyan Methodist Conference condemned the practice and when Bourne continued to hold such meetings he was expelled from the Society in 1808. It was not, however, until 1810 that the first class meeting was held at Stanley. Bourne built the first Primitive Methodist Chapel at Tunstall in 1811 and the name of the Society was finally adopted the following year. From this the movement spread throughout the country, particularly in industrial areas. In the following listings, chapels are identified with the branch of Methodism to which they were affiliated in about 1837 and any previous affiliation may not necessarily be noted. For example, in 1837 there was a Methodist New Connexion Chapel at Amblecote in the parish of Kingswinford. This had, however, initially been built by the Wesleyans in 1831, but had been sold to the New Connexion in 1836. Some chapels have foundation dates which preceed the formation of their particular branch of Methodism. This would indicate that the congregation was initially Wesleyan, but adopted one of the division prior to 1837.

Over the last few years, a large quantity of Methodist material has been transferred to local libraries. Amongst these are Minute and Account Books which can be of value to the genealogist. Whilst such items are not included here unless of direct value to the genealogist, such records should not be ignored. For example, the deposit of West Street Wesleyan Sunday School at Leek includes an Admission Register from 1804 to 1844. Attention should also be drawn to the fact that many of the deposited Methodist registers are likely to be Circuit registers covering more than one chapel. This is not always obvious from the description of the register and unfortunately, a check of the areas covered by each has not been possible.

Works of reference: "Old Glory: South Staffordshire Methodism" Henry Bunting undated; "Sketches of Early Methodism in the Black Country" Honest Munchen 1871; "Early Methodism in Staffordshire" Joseph Jones, undated; "Black Country Methodism" A C Pratt 1891.

INDEPENDENT METHODISTS

One Circuit, Burslem, existed in 1837, but no information on any chapels is available.

METHODIST NEW CONNEXION

In 1837 there were only two Staffordshire Circuits at Hanley (Shelton) and Longton. It is probable that the adjacent Circuits of Dudley in Worcestershire and Birmingham in Warwickshire may have covered some of the southern part of the County at this time. Fifty chapels have been identified of which only four registers have been surrendered. Two of these were the Circuit registers of Longton (1818) and Shelton (1797). In addition, two other registers not surrendered, Burslem (1811) and Epworth Street, Stoke-on-Trent (1813) are now deposited at the County Record Office. The earliest register, that for Cheslyn Hay, commences in 1789.

PRIMITIVE METHODISTS

In 1837 the Primitive Methodists Circuits were Burton-on-Trent, Darlaston, Leek, Lichfield, Longton, Newcastle-under-Lyme, Ramsor and Tunstall. Again, the southern part of the County may have been covered by the Birmingham West Circuit of Warwickshire. The Dudley, Worcestershire Circuit covered chapels in the parish of Kingswinford. Sixty-nine chapels have been listed, of which seven surrendered registers. These include Burton-on-Trent (1826), Ellastone (Ramsor Circuit) (1826), Longton (1834), Newcastle-under-Lyme (1824) and Tunstall (1819), the registers of which are likely to be Circuit registers. Two other early registers, Bilston (1827) held by Wolverhampton Library and Brierley Hill (1829 covering a wide area) held by Dudley Library have survived. The register for Tunstall (1819) is the oldest surviving register.

WESLEYAN METHODISTS

In 1837 three Districts covered the Staffordshire Circuits. The Birmingham and Shrewsbury District covered the Birmingham West, Dudley, Stourbridge, Walsall, Wednesbury, West Bromwich and Wolverhampton Circuits. The Macclesfield District covered the Burslem, Leek, Longton, Newcastle-under-Lyme, Stafford and Uttoxeter Circuits and the Nottingham and Derby District covered the Burton-on-Trent and Lichfield Circuits. One hundred and twenty-five Wesleyan Chapels are listed with pre-1838 origins. Twenty of these were founded in the eighteenth century, the earliest being Tipton (1750), Wednesbury (1760) and Burslem (1766). Twenty-one registers were surrendered, two of which from Tipton were classified as Worcestershire. They include registers from all the above circuit churches which are, consequently, likely to be Circuit Registers. Note that the Birmingham West (Cherry Street) Circuit Register is listed under Warwickshire, whilst those for Dudley and Stourbridge are under Worcestershire. The earliest registers are for Tunstall commencing in 1787. Two pre-1838 registers not surrendered are still in the hands of the incumbent; Ettingshall (1825) and Tutbury (1830). None of the baptismal registers have been published, although many have been microfilmed. Extracts from an account book which includes burial charges have been published for Brierley Hill by the Birmingham and Midland Society for Genealogy and Heraldry.

WESLEYAN METHODIST ASSOCIATION

Only one chapel, Hanley, has been listed. In the 1851 census, the building was said to have been erected prior to 1800. However, it has not been possible to determine if this congregation joined the Wesleyan Methodist Association in 1837 or at a later date.

MODERN METHODIST CIRCUITS

The circuits are grouped in four districts:

Birmingham District, covering the Blackheath, Lichfield, Oldbury, Tamworth and West Bromwich circuits;

Chester and Stoke-on-Trent District, covering the Biddulph and Mow Cop, Cheadle, Congleton, Leek, Market Drayton, Newcastle, Sandbach and Alsager, Stoke-on-Trent-Burslem, Burslem Mission, Hanley, Kidsgrove, Longton Mission, South Tunstall, Wolstanton and Audley Circuits;

Nottingham and Derby District, covering the Burton-on-Trent circuit;

Wolverhampton and Shrewsbury District, covering the Bilston, Bloxwich and Willenhall, Brownhills and Pelsall, Cannock Chase, Cradley Heath, Darlaston, Dudley, Gornal and Sedgley, Old Hill, Stafford, Stour Vale, Stourbridge and Brierley Hill, Telford (North), Telford (South), Tipton, Walsall, Walsall Mission, Wednesbury Mission, Wolverhampton (Darlington Street) and Wolverhampton (Trinity) Circuits.

SANDEMANIANS

A building in Tunstall was registered for Sandemanians by nine people in 1812. It was said to have met for some time. There is no information to suggest any register is still extant.

Works of reference: "History of Stoke-upon-Trent" J Ward 1842 page 93.

REGIMENTAL REGISTERS

These cover Births, Baptisms, Marriages and Deaths for the period from 1790 to 1924 and are kept in St Catherine's House London. They are the original registers kept by the various regiments. For Marriages, Deaths and Burials it is preferable, though not essential, to know the regiment. The most likely regiments for Staffordshire people were the 38th Regiment of Foot, the 80th Regiment of Foot, which joined to become the south Staffordshire Regiment, the Regiment of Foot and the 98th Regiment of Foot, which joined to become the North Staffordshire Regiment. They are now the Staffordshire Regiment (Prince of Wales')

MONUMENTAL INSCRIPTIONS

Until recently, very little work has been carried out. The County Record Office did hold a number of transcripts, but these had been done by a variety of voluntary bodies and it was suggested should be treated with caution. Over the past year or so, the Birmingham and Midland Society for Genealogy and Heraldry has been putting increasing resources into recording work. As work is completed, copies are being sent to the Society of Genealogists, the County Record Office, the Birmingham Reference Library, the incumbent if the church has not been demolished and the nearlest large local library, the Society also retaining a copy. At present, completed deposits have been made for St Lawrence Darlaston, Pinfold Street, Wesleyan Darlaston, Union Row Congregational Church, Hansdsworth, All Saints Sedgley, St Mary's RC Church, Walsall, St George, Wolverhampton, as well as for the post-1837 churches of St George Darlaston and St Andrew Handsworth.

A number of North Staffordshire inscriptions have also been recorded and deposited: St Paul Burslem, St Matthew Etruria, St John Hanley, Bethsada Methodist Church Hanley, St John Longton and St James Longton. It is anticipated that many more will be added in the near future.

NEWSPAPERS

The following newspapers with starting dates prior to 1837 cover the County.

Midland Counties Herald 1836-1933, copies at BRL
The Philanthropist 1835-1836, copies at BRL
Staffordshire Advertiser 1795+, copy at WSL; 1795-1944, copy at Holmcroft Library, Holmcroft Road, Stafford; 1795-1816, 1819-28, 1831+, copy at HPL.
Staffordshire County Herald 1831-1832, copy at HPL.
Staffordshire Gazette (Mf) 1814-1818 (few issues only), copy at NPL.
Staffordshire Mercury 1830-1891, copy at NPL.

It should be noted that the location of copies given above is by no means complete, but given only as a general indication.
The Staffordshire Record Society published, in 1968, an index to the birth, marriage and death announcements in the Staffordshire Advertiser for the period from 1795 to 1820.

DIRECTORIES AND POLL BOOKS

A number of directories deal with Staffordshire and are listed below:

1818 Pigot & Co, Staffordshire Directory. Copies at Birmingham, Brierley Hill, Hanley, Leek, Lichfield, Newcastle, Smethwick, Stafford, West Bromwich, Willenhall and Wolverhampton Libraries.

1822-1823 Pigot & Co, Staffordshire Directory. Copies at Hanley and Newcastle Libraries.

1829 Pigot & Co, Commercial Directory. Copies at Birmingham, Hanley, Stafford and William Salt Libraries.

1834 W White, History, Gazeteer & Directory of Staffordshire. Copies at Birmingham, Brierley Hill, Burton-on-Trent, Dudley, Hanley, Lichfield, Newcastle, Smethwick, Stourbridge, Tamworth, Walsall and Wolverhampton Libraries.

1841 Pigot & Co, Staffordshire Directory. Copies at Birmingham, Hanley and Stafford Libraries.

1851 W White History, Gazeteer & Directory of Staffordshire. Copies at Birmingham, Brierley Hill, Burton-on-Trent, Dudley, Hanley, Leek, Lichfield, Newcastle, Smethwick, Stafford, Stourbridge, Walsall, Willenhall, William Salt and Wolverhampton Libraries.

Again, the listing is not complete, but indicates the more important directories with know locations.

Amongst the Poll Books covering Staffordshire are:

Staffordshire 1747, copies at Birmingham and Stafford Libraries.

Lichfield 1747, copy at Stafford Library.

Staffordshire South 1835, copy at Stafford Library; 1838-39, 1839-43, copies at Birmingham Library.

Staffordshire North 1832, 1838-39 to 1861-62, copy at Birmingham Library.

PUBLISHING SOCIETIES

The Birmingham and Midland Society for Genealogy and Heraldry.
Hon Secretary Mrs P. Saul, 31 Seven Star Road, Solihull, West Midlands, B91 2BZ.

The North Staffordshire Field Club. Membership Secretary, Mrs E.M. Dodd, c/o City Central Library, Local Studies Section, Bethesda Street, Hanley, Staffordshire.

The Staffordshire Parish Register Society. Hon Secretary: A.T.C. Lavender, 91 Brenton Road, Penn, Wolverhampton, WV4 5NS.

The Staffordshire Record Society formerly the William Salt Archaeological Society. Mr D.A. Johnson, c/o The William Salt Library, Eastgate Street, Stafford.

USEFUL WORKS OF REFERENCE

The Natural History of Staffordshire, Robert Plott 1686 (Facsimile copy printed, E.J. Marton, Publishers, Manchester 1973).

A Survey of Staffordshire, Sampson Erdeswick, 1717.

The History and Antiquities of Staffordshire, Stebbing Shaw 1798-1801, two Volumes. (Facsimile copy 1976).

The Victoria County History of the County of Stafford, University of London, Institute of Historical Records, Oxford University Press, London (multi volume):

Volume I Natural History and Zoology (1968); Volume II Trades, Transport and Sports (1967); Volume III Religion (1970); Volume IV Staffordshire-Doomsday and West Cuttlestone Hundred (1958); Volume V East Cuttlestone Hundred (1959); Volume VIII Newcastle-under-Lyme, Stoke-on-Trent and the Potteries (1963); Volume XVIII Offlow Hundred (part).

Staffordshire Record Office, Cumulative Hand List Part I, Lichfield Joint Record Office, Diocesan Probate and Church Commissioners Records, Staffordshire County Council 1970.

The Registrations of Dissenting Chapels and Meeting Houses in Staffordshire 1689-1852, Barbara Donaldson, Historical Collections of Staffordshire, fourth Series, Volume III, Staffordshire Record Society 1960.

Staffordshire Estate Maps before 1840, a Handlist. Staffordshire County Record Office 1980.

West Midlands Genealogy, Audrey H. Higgs and D. Wright, West Midlands Branch of the Library Association 1966.

Some Copy Census Returns held by the West Midland Public Libraries 1973. D. Wright, West Midlands Branch of the Library Association 1973.

ABBOT's BROMLEY St Nicholas (L) (1621). OR C 1558-1912, M 1558-1968, B
1558-1870, Banns 1844-1927 (SRO). BT 1668-1859 (gaps 1671-72, 1714-
15, 1717-18, 1731-32, 1744-76, 1852-53) (LJRO). COP CMB 1558-1734
Ms (Inc), CMB 1558-1812 Ms (WSL), P/S (BT) 1755-68 (LJRO), Extr Ms (BRL),
Extr CM 1668-1859 (IGI).

ABBOT'S BROMLEY (Ind), Bethesda Chapel. f 1807.

ACTON TRUSSEL St James (L). Formerly a Chapelry to Stafford St Mary; parochially
included with Bednall. Royal Peculiar of Whittington and Baswich. OR
C 1571-1625, 1721-50, 1783-1923, M 1721-50, 1754-1836, B 1721-50, 1813-
1933, Banns 1824-73 (SRO). BT 1659-1872 (gaps 1663-72, 1672-78, 1681-
83, 1707-10, 1744-50, 1856, 1858-62) (LJRO). BT's for 1744-50 are in Bednall
whilst those for Bednall are included here for 1659-62, 1672, 1693-96, 1714-
17, 1750-56, 1798-1810. COP Extr CM 1659-1750, M 1750-1837, C 1813-
72 (IGI).

ADAMSCROFT (Wes). See under NORTON-IN-THE-MOORS.

ADBASTON St Michael (L) (601). OR CMB 1600 + (Inc). BT 1660-1856 (gaps
1686-89, 1695-99, 1721-27 (LJRO). COP CMB 1600-1727, M 1727-60 Ms
(WSL), CMB 1600-1727, M 1727-60 (I) (Ptd from Ms BMSGH), CB 1727-1839,
M 1761-1839 (I) (Ptd BMSGH), CMB 1600-1727, M 1727-60 Mf of Ms (NPL,
SG, HPL), Extr C 1600-1726, 1813-56, M 1600-1760 (IGI), M
1600-1838 (SMI).

ALDRIDGE St Mary (L) (1700). OR CMB 1660+ (Inc), Banns 1824-71 (SRO). BT
1660-1856 (gaps 1711-14, 1730-32, 1744-47, 1751-75, 1853, M 1762-70 (LJRO).
COP 1654-1749 Ms (SG), M 1654-1750 (Boyd Misc), M 1654-1749 (SMI), Extr
C 1660-1856 M 1660-1837 (IGI). See also under GREAT BARR St Margaret.

ALDRIDGE. A nonconformist chapel was registered in 1822, but no denomination
was given.

ALREWAS All Saints (L) (1607). Peculiar of the Prebend of Alrewas and Weeford.
OR C 1547-59, 1813-82, M 1560-1902, B 1813-69, Banns 1823-1941 (SRO).
BT 1664-1852 (gaps 1672-75, 1677-78, 1702-04, 1735-38 (LJRO). COP CMB
1547-1795 Ms (WSL), Extr C 1664-1852, M 1664-1735, 1738-1837 (IGI).

ALREWAS (S of F), Fradley, reg 1706.

ALREWAS (Prim Meth). reg 1828.

ALREWAS (Wes). f 1802.

ALSTONFIELD alias Alstonefield St Peter (L) (4827). OR C 1538-1849, M 1538-
1665, 1638-1837, B 1538-1903, Banns 1823-32 (SRO). BT 1661-1868 (gaps
M 1672, CMB 1673-75 (LJRO). COP CMB 1538-1812 (Ptd SPRS), M 1538-
1812 (SMI, CMI), Extr C 1538-1868, M 1542-1837 (IGI). See also under ELKSTONE,
LONGNOR, QUARNFORD and WARSLOW.

ALSTONFIELD (Prim Meth), Fawfield Head, Hulme End, erected 1834. Another
at Milldale erected 1835.

ALSTONFIELD (Wes), Bethel Chapel, erected 1801. Another at Hollinsclough,
reg 1797 and another at Newstone, erected 1816.

ALTON St Peter alias Alveton (L) (2391). OR C 1681-1746, 1762-1835, M 1681-
1746, 1754-1837, B 1681-1746, 1762-1868 (SRO), C 1836+ (Inc). BT 1676-
1852 (gaps 1679/80, CB 1758-62, 1770-73, 1846 (LJRO). COP Extr C 1767-
1852, M 1676-1837 (IGI). See also under COTTON.

ALTON (RC), Alton Towers. OR C 1820+ M 1837+ (Inc).

ALTON (Ind), Provinces Chapel, reg 1807. OR ZC 1811-37 (PRO). COP ZC 1811-
37 Mf (SRO), Extr C 1811-14, 1828-37 (IGI).

ALTON (Meth NC), Moat Hall, reg 1801.

ALTON (Prim Meth). reg 1826

ALVETON. See under ALTON.

AMBLECOTE. See under KINGSWINFORD.

ANSLOW. See under ROLLESTON.

ANSLOW LEES. See under ROLLESTON.

ARLEY UPPER alias Over Arley, St Peter (L) (735). Peculiar of the Dean and
    Chapter of Lichfield, transferred to Worcs.dioc.1905. OR CMB 1564+ (Inc).
    BT 1672-1861 (gaps 1675-81, 1687-90, 1696-99, 1707-14, 1717-19, 1732-
    35, 1741-44, 1750-53, 1857) (LJRO). COP CMB 1564-1812 ptd (WPRS),
    CMB 1564-1964 Mf (WRO), Extr C 1564-1812, M 1564-1812 (IGI-under Worcestershire).

ARMITAGE alias Armitage with Handsacre, St John Baptist (L) (977). Peculiar
    of the Prebend of Handsacre and Armitage. OR C 1673-1911, M 1673-1837,
    B 1673-1812, Banns 1854-1955 (SRO), B 1812+ (Inc). BT 1623-1861 (gaps
    1626-63, 1666-75, 1721-24, 1744-47, 1828 (LJRO). COP CMB 1623-1812
    (SPRS), CMB 1623-1837 Ms (WSL), M 1638-1837 (SMI), M 1623-1812 (CMI),
    Extr C 1623-1862, M 1813-40 (IGI). See also under BRERETON.

ARMITAGE (Ind). reg 1820. OR C 1821-37 (PRO). COP C 1821-37 Mf (SRO),
    Extr C 1821-37 (IGI).

ARMITAGE (Wes), Handsacre. reg 1828.

ASHLEY St John the Baptist (L) (825). OR C 1551-1936, M 1551-1912, B 1551-
    1979, Banns 1823-1971 (SRO), BT 1661-1875 (gaps 1800-04, 1836-43, 1859-
    63, 1870-74) (LJRO). COP CMB 1551-1742, M 1754-1812 Ms (WSL), CMB
    1551-1733 Mf (HPL,NPL), CMB 1551-1742 Mf (SG), M 1551-1742 (SMI),
    Extr C 1551-1857, M 1551-1850 (IGI).

ASHLEY (RC). reg 1791. OR CM 1825+ Confirmations 1829 (Inc).

ASHLEY (Prim Meth), Hookgate, reg 1834 but origins may date back to 1790.

ASTON (RC). See under STONE.

ASTON-BY-STONE (RC). See under STONE.

AUDLEY St James (L) (3617). OR C 1538-1868, M 1538-1875, B 1538-1867, Banns
    1823-57 (SRO). BT 1674-1857 (gaps M 1674-76, 1682/3, CM 1691-93, B
    1692-93, M 1776-82, (LJRO) (also includes Talk entries). COP CMB 1538-
    1712 (I) ptd (BMSGH), CMB 1538-1785 Ms (BRL), M 1538-1712 (SMI), Extr
    C 1674-1857, M 1676-1838, (IGI). See also under TALKE-O'-TH-HILL.

AUDLEY (Ind), Halmerend. f 1817.

AUDLEY (Wes), erected 1810. Two other chapels at Halmerend, one erected
    1809, another erected 1836. Another chapel at Knowle End, Wedgewood
    Place, erected 1833. See also under TALKE-O'-TH-HILL.

BAGNAL St Chad, Chapelry to Bucknall (L). OR C 1800-73, M 1802-1914, B
    1834-1906, Banns 1834-1906 (SRO). No earlier registers known. BT C 1758-
    62 included with Stoke-on-Trent, 1776-91 and 1812 with Bucknall (LJRO).
    COP C 1800-12 Ptd (SPRS-Bucknall cum Bagnall Volume), Extr C 1800-
    12 (IGI).

BAGNALL (Ind), Tomkin Chapel, erc 1836.

BARLASTON St John the Baptist (L) (514). OR C 1575-1914, M 1575-1933, B
    1575-1893, Banns 1823-1921 (SRO). BT 1674-1868 (gaps 1762-66, 1770-
    73, M 1860-68) (LJRO). COP C 1573-1812, M 1598-1812, B 1551-60, 1573-
    1812 ptd (SPRS), Extr C 1573-1868, M 1573-1611, 1805-68 (IGI)

BARLASTON. A Nonconformist chapel was registered in 1810, but no denomination
was given.

BARR GREAT. See under GREAT BARR.

BARR PERRY. See under PERRY BARR.

BARTON-UNDER-NEEDWOOD St James (L), Chapelry to Tatenhill. OR CMB
1571+ (Inc), Banns 1828-1881 (SRO). BT 1660-1869 (LJRO). COP CMB 1571-
1812 (I) ptd (SPRS), M 1571-1812 (SMI, CMI), Extr C 1571-1868 (IGI).

BARTON-UNDER-NEEDWOOD (Prim Meth), erected 1828.

BARTON-UNDER-NEEDWOOD (Wes), erected 1828.

BASFORD (S of F). See under CHEDDLETON.

BASWICH alias Berkswich, Baswich with Walton, Holy Trinity (L) (1329). Peculiar
of the Prebend of Whittington and Baswich. OR C 1601-1937, M 1601-1974,
B 1601-1909, Banns 1754-1812, 1823-43, Certs of M 1749-1816 (SRO). BT
1662-1883 (gaps 1670-72, 1707-10, 1735-38, 1853, MB 1880-83) (LJRO).
COP CMB 1601-1812 Ptd (SPRS), M 1601-1812 (CMI), Extr CM 1601-1812
(IGI).

BEDNALL, latterly All Saints, Chapelry to St Mary's Stafford. Parochially included
with Acton Trussel. OR CMB 1704-50, C 1783-1886, M 1754-1837, B 1783-
1812, Banns 1823-84 (SRO), B 1813+ (Inc). BT 1678-1875 (gaps 1681-84,
1735-38, 1861). Included with Acton Trussel are 1659-62, 1672, 1693-96,
1714-17, 1750-56, 1798-1810. Acton Trussell BT's included for 1744-50
(LJRO). COP Extr C 1678-1875, M 1679-1746, 1759-1810, 1813-36 (IGI).

BELLAMORE (RC). See under TIXALL.

BERKSWICH. See under BASWICH.

BETLEY St Margaret (L) (870). OR C 1538-1802, 1813-1919, M 1538-1950, B
1538-1803, 1812-1950, Banns 1824-1964 (gaps CMB 1602/3, 1623-31, 1633-
52), regs 1737, 1744-66 include burials outside the parish (SRO). BT 1673-
1859 (gaps 1712-13, 1763-65, 1771-72, 1849-50) (LJRO). COP CMB 1538-
1812 ptd (SPRS), M 1538-1812 (SMI, CMI), Extr C 1538-1802, 1813-59, M
1538-1848 (IGI).

BETLEY (Wes), erected 1808.

BIDDULPH St Lawrence (L) (1987). OR C 1558-1902, M 1558-1900, B 1558-1906,
(gap 1640-53), Banns 1786-1901 (SRO). BT 1661-1868 (gaps 1673, 1682-
93, no M after 1837). COP CMB 1558-1794, M 1794-1812 Ms (WSL), CMB
1558-1640, 1654-1754, M 1754-1812 (Mf SG), CMB 1558-1794, M 1794-1812
(I) Mf of Ms (NPL), CMB 1558-1755 Mf of Ms (HPL), Extr C 1559-1670,
1685-1867, M 1559-1856 (IGI), M 1558-1812 (SMI).

BILSTON St Leonard (L). Chapelry to Wolverhampton until 19th century. Royal
Peculiar of Wolverhampton. OR C 1684-1951, M 1747-54, 1841-1949, B
1727-1955 (gaps C 1691-93, B 1741-46) (SRO), C 1694-1746, B 1727-40 are
entered in the Churchwardens & Constables Account Books 1669-1703 and
1704-33 (SRO). The right to perform marriages was withdrawn in 1754
following litigation from Wolverhampton St Peter. BT 1799-1835 (gap 1827).
No marriages recorded (marriages celebrated at Wolverhampton and entered
in their registers and BT's) (LJRO). COP CB 1684-1746 ptd (SPRS), C 1747-
60, M 1747-60, M 1747-54, B 1727-47 Mf (SG), CB 1684-1760 Ms (WSL),
CB 1684-1760 Mf (HPL), Extr C 1684-1746, 1801-35 (IGI), M 1684-1786
(SMI).

BILSTON St Mary, Oxford Street, erected 1830. Royal Peculiar of Wolverhampton.
OR C 1848-1951, M 1848-1941, B 1848-1975 (SRO).

BILSTON (RC), Church of the Most Holy Trinity, Oxford Street, erected 1833. OR C 1834+ M 1835+ (Inc).

BILSTON (Bapt), Wood Street, f 1798.

BILSTON (Ind), Oxford Street, f 1760. OR ZC 1785-1837 (PRO). COP ZC 1785-1837 Mf (SRO), Extr C 1783-1837 (IGI).

BILSTON (Meth NC), erected 1835.

BILSTON (Prim Meth), High Street, f 1827. OR C 1827-1907, 1914-33 (WoPL).

BILSTON (Wes), Swan Bank, Oxford Street, f 1795 in Temple Street, this chapel being erected 1824. OR ZC 1816-37, B 1823-37 includes Cann Lane and Ettingshall Road (PRO), C 1816-1909, B 1823-1954 (WoPL), Class books giving names and addresses 1821-27, 1831-35 (WoPL) Sunday School admissions 1813-21 (WoPL). COP C 1816-37 (IGI-listed as Cann Lane and Ettingshall Road Wes).

BILSTON (Wes), Bradley, erected 1806. OR B 1843-92 (Inc). Another chapel at Moxley was erected 1837.

BILSTON, Bradley. A nonconformist chapel was registered in 1810, but no denomination was given.

BLITHFIELD St Leonard (L) (468). OR C 1538-1650, 1813-1900, M 1538-1642, 1754-1856, B 1538-1645 1813-1961. (SRO), C 1650-1812, M 1642-1812, B 1645-1812 (missing). BT 1693-1877 (gaps 1747-51, 1870) (LJRO). COP Extr C 1693-1877, M 1741-1844 (IGI), C 1538-1650, 1658-1812 M 1539-1642, 1658-1753, B 1538-1645, 1658-1812, CMB 1538-1650 (I), CMB 1701-1812 (SRO).

BLOOMFIELD (Wes). See under TIPTON.

BLORE RAY St Bartholomew (L) (354). OR C 1558-1935, M 1558-1944 B 1558-1812, Banns 1784-1974 (few entries 1642-57) (SRO), B 1812+ (Inc). BT 1665-1872 (gaps 1730-32, 1766-70), 1677-79 included in terriers (LJRO). COP C 1558-1640, 1657-1812 Ms (WSL), Extr C 1813-72 (IGI).

BLORE (Prim Meth), Swinscoe, erected 1835.

BLOXWICH All Saints (L). Chapelry to Walsall until 1842. OR CMB 1733+ (Inc). Between 1669 and 1675 it was the custom to enter Bloxwich baptisms separately in the Walsall registers. Bloxwich baptisms and burials commence in 1733, but there is a duplicate volume amongst the Walsall registers where baptisms for Bloxwich commence in 1721. Note there are only six marriages in total. BT 1733-1872 (gaps 1741-44, 1761-62, C 1786-95, 1795-1800, M 1843-69, 1673-75 and 1786-95 are with Walsall (LJRO). COP C 1721-30, 1733-91, M 1736, 1737, 1739, 1746, B 1733-91 Ms (SG, WSL, LJRO, WPL), Extr M 1730-46, 1843-69 (IGI).

BLOXWICH (RC), St Thomas the Apostle, Harden Lane, erected 1801. OR 1805-29, M 1807-29, D 1807-29, Confirms 1808 (DA). COP C 1805-29 (IGI).

BLOXWICH (Wes), f 1795. First chapel was built at Short Heath in 1795 and the New Chapel at Big Green in 1832.

BLURTON St John the Baptist (L), Chapel to Trentham until 1831. OR C 1813-1950, M 1754-70, 1842-1950, B 1828-1967, Banns 1900-78 (SRO). No earlier regs. BT 1814-38. No separate earlier BT's, but the following are included with Trentham: C 1732-33, 1738-50, 1771-76, 1786-90, 1813-21 (LJRO). COP B 1820-1921 (HPL), Extr C 1814-38 (IGI).

BLYMHILL St Mary (L) (566). OR C 1561-1837, M 1561-1837 B 1561-1878, Banns 1754-1817, 1823-71 (SRO). BT 1661-1868 (gaps 1663, 1667, 1668), years 1762-66, 1770-73 listed in terriers. (LJRO). COP CMB 1561-1812 (I) ptd (SPRS), M 1561-1812 (SMI, CMI), Extr C 1561-1868, M 1561-1837 (IGI).

BLYTHE MARSH (Wes). See under DILHORNE

BOBBINGTON Holy Cross (L) (426). Peculiar Deanery of Bridgnorth, transferred
to Hereford Diocese in 1846. OR C 1571-1812, M 1571-1837, B 1571-1812
(SRO), CB 1813+ (Inc). BT 1636-1812 (BL), 1813-31 (LJRO). COP CMB
1572-1812 Ms (WSL), CMB (BT) 1662-1812 Ms (BRL), M 1651-1812 (Boyd
Misc), Extr C 1813-31 (IGI).

BOBBINGTON (Wes), Gospel Ash, erected 1830.

BRADELEY All Saints (sometimes Bradeley by Stafford) (L) (75). OR C 1538-
1940, M 1538-1944, B 1538-1895, Banns 1824-1947 (SRO). BT 1636-1867
(gaps 1636-76, 1853-55, 1865-67). COP CMB 1538-1780 (I) Ms (WSL), CMB
1598-1681 Mf (SRO), Extr CMB 1538-1700 (SG), M 1538-1780 (SMI), Extr
C 1636-38, 1677-1765, 1776-1864, M 1636-38, 1677-1864 (IGI). See also
under BILSTON.

BRADLEY-IN-THE-MOORS All Saints (L) (780). OR CMB 1678+ (Inc). BT 1674-
1867 (gap 1776-91) (LJRO). COP CMB 1674-1812 (I) ptd (SPRS), M 1674-
1812 (CMI), Extr C 1674-1811, 1813-68, M 1679-1851 (IGI).

BRAMSHALL St Lawrence (L) (170). OR CMB 1588+ (at Uttoxeter). BT 1673-
1889 (gaps 1685-90, 1758-62, 1766-73) (LJRO). COP CMB 1587-1812 Ms
(WSL), CMB 1588-1812 Mf (SRO), Extr C 1673-1758, 1774-1877, M 1673-
1812, 1815-36 (IGI).

BRANSTON (Ind), see under BURTON-ON-TRENT.

BRERETON St Michael, erected 1837. Mostly in Rugeley parish, partly in parishes
of Armitage and Longdon, becoming an independent parish in 1843 (L).
OR 1843+ (Inc). BT 1843-71 (LJRO).

BRERETON (Ind), reg 1828. May possibly have been a meeting house and not
a chapel.

BRERETON (Wes), reg 1810. OR M 1915-61 (SRO).

BRETHILL (Prim Meth). See under ROWLEY REGIS.

BREWOOD St Mary (L) (3799). Peculiar of the Dean of Lichfield. OR CMB 1562+
(Inc). BT 1618-1859 (gaps 1619-62, 1672-75, 1698-1702, 1706-11, 1747-50,
1769-54, CM 1681-95, CB 1804-10) (LJRO). COP CMB 1562-1649 ptd (SPRS),
CB 1653-1784, M 1653-1768 Ms (WSL), M 1562-1649 (CMI), M 1562-1768
(SMI), Extr C 1561-1650, 1663-1858, M 1561-1645, 1663-1803, 1813-40 (IGI).
See also under COVEN.

BREWOOD (RC), Chillington, Blackladies, reg 1791. The Chaplain from Chillington
Hall moved to Blackladies in 1787 and this remained the chief Catholic
Chapel until the opening of Brewood Church in 1844. The Chapel at Chillington
Hall was demolished in 1787 when further rebuilding took place. OR C
1720-37, 1762-95, M 1720-31 (Inc). COP 1720/1-37, 1762-70, M 1720-31
ptd (SPRS), C 1771-95 ptd (Staffs Cath Hist 15. 1975), M 1720-31 (SMI, CMI)
Extr C 1721-70, M 1721-31 (IGI).

BREWOOD (RC) Long Birch, regd 1791. This was a Dower House of Chillington
and the residence of the Vicars Apostolic until 1804. Though they had Chaplains
who administered to the local Catholics, entries were probably made in
the Chillington register.

BREWOOD (Ind), regd 1803. OR ZC 1810-37 (PRO). COP ZC 1810-37 Mf (CRO),
C 1810-37 (IGI).

BRIERLEY HILL St Michael. Chapelry in the parish of Kingswinford until 1848
(L). OR C 1766+ M 1837+ B 1766+ (Inc). Note some marriages were performed
before 1837 and these are included in the registers of St Mary's Kingswinford,
Banns 1766-81 (DPL listed under Holy Trinity, Wordsley). BT 1766-1864
(gaps 1781-86, 1841, 1846-57, 1859-63, CB 1766-81) (LJRO). Many entries

for 1776-81 have no dates. COP Extr C 1776-1864 (IGI).

BRIERLEY HILL (Part Bapt), Nine Locks, Meeting Lane, f 1776. In 1805 a new
chapel was erected in Meeting Lane with its own burial ground, moving
to a new chapel in South Street in 1853. OR Z 1793-1836 (PRO) listed as
Kingswinford, Brettell Lane), Min. Bks. with members list 1798, 1800 (DPL),
Min. Bk. 1826-53 with notes of admissions and emigrations (DPL). COP Z
1793-1836 Mf (SRO) Extr Z 1778-1836 (IGI listed as Kingswinford, Brettell
Lane, Baptist).

BRIERLEY HILL (Ind), Mill Lane, erected 1839. f c. 1830 at Round Oak, erected
c. 1834 to about 1837 at Harts Hill, Brierley Hill. No registers before 1837
known. Another Independant chapel at Brockmoor erected 1827.

BRIERLEY HILL (Meth NC), Brockmoor, erected 1827, bought by Welseyans in
1838. OR (Wes) C 1845-1965 (DPL). No earlier known registers. Another
Meth NC chapel at Quarry Bank, Mount Pleasant erected 1836.

BRIERLEY HILL (Prim Meth), Quarry Bank f 1830. First chapel built in Sheffield
Street 1830, a new one in Rose Hill in 1845 and another in New Street in
1860.

BRIERLEY HILL (Prim Meth), Round Oak, later called Bent Street erected 1826.
OR C 1829-1944, B 1902-46 (DPL). Register from 1829 is probably a Circuit
register and includes Baptisms in Smethwick, Cradley Heath, Rowley Regis
and Kingswinford. COP C 1829-39 Ms (BRL, SG, BMSGH, DPL) another
chapel at Quarry Bank, Sheffield Street, erected 1830.

BRIERLY HILL (Wes), Bank Street, originally known as Gorsty Bank. f 1825.
OR C 1844-1973 (DPL). COP B 1833-84 (names only given for 1833-53)
ptd (BMSCH - Burial entries and pew rents from account book 1833-84).
Another Chapel at Bromley erected 1823 and another at Quarry Bank, Mount
Pleasant erected 1828, which register of baptisms commence in 1844 (Inc).

BROCKMOOR. See under BRIERLEY HILL.

BROD (Part Bapt). See under WALSALL.

BROMLEY (Wes). See under BRIERLEY HILL.

BROMLEY KING's. See under KING's BROMLEY

BROMLEY REGIS. See under KING's BROMLEY.

BROMSTEAD HEATH (Ind). See under GNOSALL, BROMSTEAD HEATH.

BROMWICH WEST. See under WEST BROMWICH.

BROOME St Peter. Chapelry to Clent (L) (110). Transferred to Worcestershire
c 1850. OR CMB 1666+ Banns 1824+ (Inc). BT 1613-1873 (gaps 1614-15,
1617-18, 1620-24, 1641-60) (WRO).. COP CMB 1616-1873 Mf of BT (WRO),
Extr C 1785-1877 (IGI).

BROWN EDGE (Wes). See under NORTON-IN-THE-MOORS.

BROWNHILLS (Ind). See under NORTON CANES.

BUCKNALL alias Bucknall-cum-Bagnall. Chapelry built 1718, to Stoke-on-Trent.
Made into a parish with Bagnall in 1807. (L) OR C 1758-1935, M 1765-1936,
B 1763-1947 (SRO). BT 1758-1855 (gaps 1773-76, M 1759-62) (LJRO). Also
includes some Bagnall entries. M 1759-62 with Stoke-on-Trent. COP C
1762-1812, M 1765-1812, B 1763-1812 ptd (SPRS), M 1765-1812 (SMI, CMI),
Extr C 1762-1855, M 1765-1848 (IGI). See also under BAGNALL.

BUCKNALL (Meth NC), f 1812.

BUCKPOOL (?). See under KINGSWINFORD.

BURNTWOOD Christ Church (L). Chapelry to Lichfield. Erected 1820, becoming a parish in 1845. Peculiar to the Dean of Lichfield. OR 1820+ (Inc). BT 1826-72 (LJRO). COP Extr C 1826-72 (IGI).

BURSLEM St John the Baptist (L) (12,714). Chapelry to Stoke-on-Trent. OR 1637-93, 1702-1888, M 1637-93, 1702-1884, B 1637-93, 1702-1880, legible from 1639 only. (SRO). No earlier regs extant. BT 1660-1855 (gaps 1673-75, 1708-10, 1714-17, M 1837-55), 1744-47 with terriers (SRO). COP CMB 1578-1812 ptd (SPRS), M 1578-1812 (CMI), Extr C 1581-1856, M 1578-61, 1761-1837 (IGI).

BURSLEM St Paul. District Chapelry, erected 1830. OR C 1831-1937, M 1845-1951, B 1831-1958, Banns 1845-1966 (SRO). BT 1831-69 (gaps 1859-60, 1868, no M) (LJRO). COP Extr C 1831-53, 1857-69 (IGI).

BURSLEM (RC), St Peter's, Cobridge. Erected 1780. OR C 1797+ M 1838+ Confirms 1815+ (DA).

BURSLEM (Bapt), f 1791. OR Z 1808-37 (PRO). COP Extr Z 1791-1837 (IGI).

BURSLEM (Ind), f 1821. A chapel was built in Queen Street 1837 replacing one called Nile Street formerly the Salem Chapel. OR ZC 1823-37 (PRO). COP ZC 1826-31 Mf (HPL), Extr C 1823-31 (IGI).

BURSLEM (Meth), Dissenting Meeting House, reg 1766.

BURSLEM (Meth NC), Bethel Chapel, Waterloo Road, f 1799. This chapel was built in 1824, replacing the Zoar chapel in Nile Street. OR C 1811-1955 (SRO).

BURSLEM (Meth NC), Providence Chapel, Cobridge, reg 1819. This chapel was built in 1822 replacing the one in Sneyd Green. OR ZC 1867-79 (SRO), ZC 1840-1955 (SRO as United Meth).

BURSLEM (Prim Meth), Navigation Street, erected 1821. OR ZC 1823-37 (PRO). COP ZC 1823-37 Mf (HPL), Extr C 1823-37 (IGI).

BURSLEM (Wes), Hill Top Chapel, erected 1836. Also known as Burslem Sunday School. It broke away from the Wesleyans at Swann Bank in the 1830's and joined the Wes. Meth. Assoc. in 1849. OR Misc. Records of Chapel and Sunday School but no known registers (HPL). Baptismal entries for the Chapel at Longport (erected 1811) and at Sneyd Green (erected 1821) may be included in the register for Burslem Swan Bank.

BURSLEM (Wes), Swan Bank, f 1800. Circuit register before 1837. OR ZC 1800-13 (Methodist Society of Burslem and vicinity) (PRO), C 1813-32 (Wes chapels in the parish of Stoke out of Wolstanton, including Burslem, Sneyd, Green, Hanley, Tunstall, Goldenhill, Kidsgrove, Longport, Hall Green, Harriseahead and Norton) (PRO), ZC 1832-37 (Burslem Circuit, including a few baptisms in adjacent villages) (PRO). COP ZC 1800-13, C 1813-32, ZC 1832-37 (Mf HPL, NPL), Extr C 1800-37 (IGI).

BURTON-ON-TRENT St Modwen (L) (6455), Peculiar of the Prebend of Burton-on-Trent. OR CMB 1538 (Inc). BT 1663-1882 (gaps 1765-73) (LJRO). COP M 1538-1610 ptd (Burton Arch Soc Vols III & IV), Extr C 1663-1877, M 1663-1837 (IGI).

BURTON-ON-TRENT Holy Trinity, Horniglow St, erec 1824. Chapelry to St Modwen, now demolished. OR C 1824-1969, M 1844-1969, B 1826-91 (at St Modwen's), Banns 1882-1965 (BOT.PL). BL 1824-1889 (gap 1868-70) (LJRO). COP Extr C 1824-75 (IGI).

BURTON-ON-TRENT (RC), Burton Extra, erec 1806. Served from Woodlane, Yoxall. No early records were kept, but entries should be in the Woodlane registers.

BURTON-ON-TRENT (S of F), regd 1723.

BURTON-ON-TRENT (Gen Bapt), New Street, f 1824. OR Z 1825-36 (PRO). COP Z 1825-36 Mf(SRO,NPL), Ext Z 1823-36 (IGI).

BURTON-ON-TRENT (Part Bapt), at Street Chapel, later Salem Chapel, Station Street. f 1790. OR Z 1793-1814 (PRO). COP Z 1793-1836 Mf (SRO), Extr Z 1793-1826 (IGI).

BURTON-ON-TRENT (Ind), High Street, f 1662. Had small burial ground. OR ZC 1808-37 (PRO), C 1808-1966 (BOT.PL), B 1841-61 with D Cert (BOT.PL), COP ZC 1808-37 Mf(SRO), Extr C 1808-37 (IGI). Another chapel at Branston f 1804.

BURTON-ON-TRENT (Prim Meth), f 1820 in Burton Extra, replaced by a new chapel in Station Street 1829. OR ZC 1826-37 (PRO), C 1844-80 (BOT.PL). Note both of these are circuit regs. covering a wide area. COP ZC 1826-37 Mf (CRO, BOT.PL), Extr C 1826-37 (IGI).

BURTON-ON-TRENT (Wes), Horninglow Street, f 1795. OR ZC 1795-1837 (PRO), C 1837-1958 (Circuit reg) (BOT.PL). COP C 1795-1836 Mf(BOT.PL, SRO), Extr C 1795-1837 (IGI).

BUSHBURY St Mary (L) (1275). Royal Peculiar of Wolverhampton. OR C 1789-1908, M 1764-1906, B 1789-1908 Banns 1764-1823 (SRO). Note earlier regs. destroyed before 1831. BT 1662-1868 (gaps 1668-70, 1686-93, 1858-63) (LJRO). COP CMB 1560-1812 incorporating abstracts 1561-1662 and BT's 1662-1789, ptd (SPRS), CMB 1764-1812, M 1813-39 Ms (WSL), M 1560-1812 (SMI, CMI), Extr C 1561-1868, M 1561-1637, 1662-1848 (IGI).

BUSHBURY (RC), Moseley Old Hall, regd. 1791. OR C 1773+ M 1798+ Confirms 1805+ (Inc). COP C 1773+ M 1798 + Confirms 1805+ Ms (DA).

BUSHBURY (Wes), Essington, erec 1834.

BUTTERTON St Bartholomew. Chapelry to Mayfield (L). OR C 1746-1889, M 1746-1812, B 1746-1935, Banns 1754-1844 (SRO), M 1813+ (Inc). BT 1660-1864 (gaps 1708-11, 1762-66, 1770-73) (LJRO). COP Extr C 1660-1864, M 1660-1860 (IGI).

CALDEN. see under CAULDON.

CALTON St Mary. Chapelry to Waterfall (L). Became parish in 1902. OR C 1813-1915 (SRO), C 1760-92 (Chapel Clerks pocket book, Inc) BT 1809-44 (gap1840). see Waterfall for earlier records. COP C 1809-44 (IGI).

CANNOCK St Luke (L) (3116). Peculiar of the Dean and Chapter of Lichfield. OR C 1774-1811, M 1744-54, B 1744-1811 (destroyed by fire c. 1858), C 1811-1914, M 1754-1917, B 1881-1929, Banns 1809-1914 (SRO). BT 1659-1867 (gaps 1672-83, 1686-90, 1858-65). COP CB 1744-64, M 1744-54, B 1811-12 Ms (WSL, SG, Cannock PL), Index CB 1744-64, B 1811-12) (BMSGH), CMB 1660-1812 Mf of Ms-difficult to read (NPL), 1659-1770 (fragmentary) Mf of Ms (HPL), Extr C 1659-1867, M 1659-1838 (IGI).

CANNOCK (Ind), f 1815. OR ZC 1816-37 (PRO). Note in PRO list says Volume is 1816-17. COP ZC 1816-37 Mf (SRO), Extr C 1816-37 (IGI).

CANNOCK WOOD (Prim Meth), erec before 1800.

CANNOCK WOOD (Wes), erec 1834.

CARTERS GREEN (Ind). see under WEST BROMWICH.

CASTLE CHURCH. see under STAFFORD.

CAULDON St Mary & St Lawrence (L) (347). OR C 1580-1916, M 1580-1905, B 1580-1893 (SRO). BT 1666-1856 (gaps 1671-74, 1705-08, 1766-70, C 1772, 1776-80) (LJRO). COP C 1580-1869, M 1580-1837, B 1580-1856 Ms (WSL,

SG, LJRO), M 1580-1869 (includ. BT) (SMI), Extr C 1668-1856, M 1674-1837 (IGI).

CAVERSWALL St Peter (L) (1207). OR C 1552-1895, M 1552-1920, B 1552-1916 (gaps 1643-61, 1666, 1677-82, CM 1699, early years illegible), Banns 1846-61 (SRO). BT 1663-1864 (Gaps 1666-71, 1676, 1682-85, M 1766-70, 1810-12, 1843) (LJRO). COP CMB 1552-1643, 1662-1813 Ms (WSL), CMB 1559-1822 Mf(SG), CMB 1552-1813 Mf of Ms (NPL), CMB 1566-1813 Mf of Ms (HPL), Extr C 1663-1809, 1813-64, M 1663-1809, 1813-42 (IGI).

CAVERSWALL (RC), f 1811. OR C 1811+ M 1865+ (Inc). COP C 1811+ Ms (DA).

CAVERSWALL (Meth NC), Tabernacle, erec 1812. Another chapel at Fox Earth, reg 1811 and another at Werrington, reg 1812.

CAVERSWALL (Wes), erec 1809.

CHAPEL CHORLTON St Lawrence. Chapelry to Eccleshall (L). Peculiar of the Prebend of Eccleshall. OR CMB 1564-1710, 1715-1813, C 1813-91, M 1817-36, Banns 1855-1966 (SRO), B 1813+ (Inc). BT 1681-1876 (Gaps 1683-96, 1702-10, 1717-1800, 1836-47, 1849-51, 1853, 1870, 1873, 1875) (LJRO). COP Extr C 1802-76 (IGI).

CHAPEL CHORLTON (Wes), Hill Chorlton, erec 1834. OR C 1841-1962 (NPL).

CHEADLE St Giles (L) (4119). OR CMB 1567-69 (badly rubbed), CMB 1575-1670, 1674-82, 1692-1776, C 1780-1915, M 1776-1937, B 1780-1927, Banns 1814-31 (SRO). BT 1660-1856 (gap CM 1819) (LJRO). COP CM 1574-1682 Ms (WSL), CMB 1660-1757, CM 1755-80 (parchment SRO), CMB 1574-1682 Mf of MS (NPL, HPL), CMB 1754-1813 (SG), M 1574-1682 (SMI), Extr C 1660-1856, M 1660-1836 (IGI). See also under OAKAMOOR.

CHEADLE (RC). OR C 1828+ M 1833+ (Inc).

CHEADLE (Ind), Bethel Chapel, Well Street, f 1799. OR C 1800-37 (PRO). COP C 1800-37 Mf (SRO), Extr C 1800-37 (IGI).

CHEADLE (Meth NC), Zion Chapel, erec 1820. OR Cheadle entries are included in the Circuit Register. See also under LONGTON, New Street.

CHEADLE (Prim Meth), Blakely Lane, erec 1830. Another at Freehay, Heapwood Chapel, erec 1835.

CHEADLE (Wes), Chapel Street, erec 1812. OR C 1838-75 (Circuit safe, Cheadle).

CHEBSEY All Saints (L) (414). OR C 1713-32, 1813-69, M 1754-1837, B 1713-50 (SRO), CB 1813+ (Inc), No OR C 1733-1812, B 1751-1812. BT 1660-1845 (gaps 1663, 1665-66, 1671-73, 1676-80, 1730-32, 1762-66, 1839 (LJRO). COP CMB 1660-1812 ptd (SPRS), CMB 1660-1837 (BT 1660-1713) Ms (WSL), CMB 1660-1713 Mf of Ms (HPL), M 1660-1812 (SMI, CMI), Extr C 1660-1713, 1715-1845, M 1660-1837 (IGI).

CHEBSEY (S of F), Shallowford, reg 1703.

CHECKLEY St Mary & All Saints (L) (2247). OR CMB 1625+ (Inc). BT 1662-1867 (gaps 1795-1800, 1854-59) (LJRO). COP Extr C 1661-1867, M 1661-1837 (IGI).

CHECKLEY (Ind), Ebenezer Chapel, Deadman's Green, f 1808. OR ZC 1822-30 (PRO). COP ZC 1822-30 Mf (SRO), Extr C 1822-30 (IGI).

CHECKLEY (Ind), Providence Chapel, Upper Tean, f 1778. OR ZC 1803-37 (PRO). COP ZC 1803-37 Mf (SRO), Extr C 1803-37 (IGI).

CHECKLEY (Prim Meth), Hollington Heath, Commonside, Great Gate, erec 1823.

CHECKLEY (Wes), erec 1833.

CHEDDLETON St Edward (L) (1664). OR C 1696-1947, M 1696-1946, B 1696-1879 (SRO). BT 1676-1829 (gaps 1693-96, 1698-1701, 1800-05) (LJRO). COP CMB(BT) 1676-1820 Ms (WSL), B 1879-1907 Ms (WSL), Extr M 1813-29 (IGI). See also under WETLEY ROCKS.

CHEDDLETON (S of F), Basford. Burial ground, deeds datd 1667 but probably unused by 1841.

CHEDDLETON (Wes), erec 1822.

CHELL (Prim Meth), see under WOLSTANTON.

CHESHIRE & STAFFORDSHIRE (S of F). Quarterly Meeting. OR Z 1783-1836, M 1768-92, 1795-1837, B 1783-1837 (PRO). M.Lics 1672-1854, Sufferings 1665-1854, Regs 1668-1837 (ChRO). COP Digests Z 1647/8-1837, M 1655-1837, B 1655-1837 containing some Staffs entries, ZMB 1688-1837, a supplementary reg. devoted mainly to Staffs entries (ChRO).

CHESLYN HAY. extra parochial. In 1846 joined with Great Wyrley to form a new ecclesiastical parish of St Mark.

CHESLYN HAY (Meth NC), Salem Chapel f 1778. OR ZC 1789-1837 (PRO). COP ZC 1821-1837 Mf (SRO), ZC 1789-1837 Ms (Inc), Extr C 1789-1837 (IGI).

CHESTERTON. See under WOLSTANTON.

CHILCOTE St Matthew (formerly Derbyshire, now Leicestershire). Chapelry to Clifton Campville (L). OR C 1595-1812, MB 1595-1734 (SRO), C 1812+ MB 1734+ (Inc). BT 1660-1864 (gaps 1726-30, 1786-1805, 1810-12, 1837, 1855-63, MB in Clifton Campville BT's (LJRO). COP Extr C 1660-1786, 1805-09, 1813-60 (IGI).

CHILLINGTON (RC). See under BREWOOD, CHILLINGTON, BLACKLADIES.

CHORLTON. See under CHAPEL CHORLTON.

CHORLTON HILL (Wes). See under CHAPEL CHORLTON.

CHORLTON MOSS (Prim Meth), see under NEWCASTLE-UNDER-LYME.

CHURCH EATON St Editha (L) (922). OR C 1538-1928, M 1538-1845, B 1538-1928, Banns 1824-87 (SRO). BT 1660-1854 (gap 1841-53). COP CMB 1538-1812 (with High Offley) Ms (WSL) ptd (BMSGH), M 1538-1812 (SMI), Extr CM 1660-1854 (IGI).

CLENT St Leonard (L) (922). Detached member of Staffordshire transferred to Worcestershire c. 1850. OR CMB 1561-1625, 1637+ Banns 1754-89 (Inc). BT 1612-1916 (gaps 1615-20, 1622-26, 1641-43, 1645-60, CB 1774-85) (WRO). COP CMB 1562-1812 (I) Ms (WRO), Extr C 1612-1700 (IGI with Worcestershire). See also under BROOME AND ROWLEY REGIS.

CLENT (Bapt), Holy Cross, f 1802. Transferred to Worcestershire c. 1850. OR Z 1807-36 (PRO). COP Extr Z 1807-36 (IGI under Staffordshire).

CLENT (Wes), f 1817. Transferred to Worcestershire c1850.

CLIFTON CAMPVILLE St Andrew (L) (801). OR C 1662-1862, M 1662-1837, B 1662-1865, Banns 1824-1915 (SRO). BT 1664-1867. COP Extr C 1664-1866, M 1664-1805, 1810-37 (IGI). See also under CHILCOTE AND HARLASTON.

COBERMARE (Prim Meth). See under STOKE-ON-TRENT.

COBRIDGE. See under BURSLEM.

CODSALL St Nicholas (L) (1115). Royal Peculiar of Tettenhall. OR C 1587-1953, M 1587-1957, B 1587-1948, Banns 1754-1811 (SRO). BT 1673-1855

(gaps 1679-86, 1693-96, 1699-1709, 1712-14, 1717-1800) (LJRO). COP
CB 1587-1812, M 1587-1843 ptd (SPRS), M 1587-1843 (SMI, CMI), Extr
C 1587-1857, M 1587-1844 (IGI).

CODSALL (Wes), erec 1825.

COLEHILL (Unit). See under TAMWORTH.

COLTON St Mary (L) (675). OR CMB 1647+ (Inc). BT 1660-1856 (gap 1766-
70) (LJRO). COP Extr C 1660-1857, M 1660-1835 (IGI).

COLWICH St Michael (L) (1918). Peculiar of the Prebend of Colwich. OR
C 1590-1859, M 1590-1958, B 1590-1872, Banns 1793-1807, 1889-1963
(SRO). M Certs 1759-1806 (SRO). BT 1659-1871 (gaps 1670-72, 1678-81,
1693-94, 1869-70) (LJRO). COP CB 1590-1803, M 1590-1790 Ms (WSL),
CB 1590-1803, M 1590-1790 Mf of Ms (HPL), Extr CM 1659-1871 (IGI).
See also under FRADSWELL.

COLWICH (RC), Chapel of Mount Paislon, erec 1837. A Benedictine Priory of
Nuns. The chapel is private and no records are kept.

COPPENHALL St Lawrence (L). CHapelry to Penkridge. Royal Peculiar of
Penkridge. OR C 1678-1812, M 1684-1837 (only 9 entries) (SRO), C 1812+
(Inc). BT C 1762-1859 (LJRO), burials at Penkridge. COP CM 1678-1837
Ms (WSL), M 1678-1837 (SMI), Extr C 1762-1859 (IGI).

COPPIA (Part Bapt). See under SEDGLEY.

COPPICE (Part Bapt). See under SEDGLEY.

COSELEY Christ Church. Chapelry to Sedgley until 1832 when it became
a parish, erec 1830. (L). OR CMB 1830+ (DPL). BT 1830-56 (gap 1854-
55) (LJRO). COP C 1830-56 (IGI).

COSELEY (Part Bapt), Dark House Chapel, f 1783. OR Z 1791-1837 (PRO).
Register Z 1786-1822 with a few later entries (Inc), B 1823+ (Inc). COP
Z 1791-1837 Ms (DPL), Z 1822-37 Mf (SRO), Extr Z 1791-1837 (IGI).

COSELEY (Bapt), Providence Chapel, f 1809. OR Z & namings 1810-37 (PRO),
B 1889-1967 (DPL). COP namings 1810-37 Ms (DPL), 1809-37 Mf (SRO),
Extr Z 1803-37 (IGI).

COSELEY (Unit), previously Presb., Old Meeting, f 1662. OR Z 1779-1837,
B 1804-37 (PRO). COP C 1779-1837, B 1804-37 Ms (DPL), ZC 1779-1837,
B 1804-37 Mf (SRO), Extr C 1792-1815, 1827-37 (IGI).

COSELEY (Wes), erec 1829.

COTES HEATH St James. Chapelry to Eccleshall until formed into a parish
in 1844, erec 1833 (L). OR 1844+ (SRO). BT 1844-73 (gaps 1869-73) (LJRO).

COTON END (Ind), Ebenezer Chapel. See GNOSALL.

COTTON St John the Baptist, Chapelry to Alton, erec 1795 (L). OR c1795-
1807 included in regs. of Alton, 1918+ (SRO). BT No registers kept, see
ALTON.

COVEN St Paul, lic 1836, 1857. Chapelry to Brewood until 1858 (L). OR CMB
1857+ (Inc). BT 1868 (LJRO).

COVEN (Wes), parish of Brewood, reg 1826.

CRADLEY FORGE. See under KINGSWINFORD.

CRADLEY HEATH. See under ROWLEY REGIS.

CRESWELL (ex paroch) (11) 2 miles from Stafford. Church in ruins by 1930.

CRESSWELL (RC). See under DRAYCOTT-IN-THE-MOORS.

CROXALL St John the Baptist (L) (29). Was in Derbyshire until 1894. OR CMB (?)1586+ (Inc). BT 1651-1864 (gap 1811-12) (LJRO). COP CMB 1586-1812 Ms (SG), CMB 1586-93, 1616-1812 Ms (Derby PL), Extr C 1586-1812, M 1587-1810, 1813-55 (IGI - listed under Derbyshire). See also under EDINGALE.

CROXDEN St Laurence (L) (272). OR CB 1673-1812, M 1673-1837 (SRO), CB 1812+ (Inc). BT 1674-1867 (gaps 1706-07, 1766-70, 1861, 1865) (LJRO). COP CMB 1674-1812(I) ptd (SPRS), M 1674-1812 (CMI), Extr C 1674-1856, M 1674-1836 (IGI).

CROXTON St Paul. Chapel to Eccleshall becoming a parish in 1857, erec 1832(L).

DARLASTON St Lawrence (L) (6647). OR C 1539-1842, M 1539-1855, B 1539-1839, Banns 1754-1834 (SRO). BT 1660-1844 (gaps 1693, M 1762-76, 1772-75, C 1782-90, 1801-04, 1836-42, 1845-52) (LJRO). COP CMB 1539-1836 Ms (WSL), Extr C 1660-1844, M 1660-1835 (IGI).

DARLASTON (Ind Calv), erec before 1800.

DARLASTON (Prim), Bill Street, erec 1837.

DARLASTON (Wes), Bethel Chapel, erec 1800. Note that the register for Springhead, Wednesday (Wes) may include some Darlaston references.

DARLASTON (Wes), Pinfold Street, erec 1810. OR ZC 1832-37, B 1833-37 (PRO), C 1837-50, B 1853-92 (WaPL), Burial account 1833+ (WaPL). Note that the register for Springhead, Wednesbury (Wes) may include some early Darlaston entries. COP ZC 1832-37, B 1833-37 Mf (SRO, WaPL), Extr C 1832-37 (IGI).

DARLASTON (Wes), Fallings Heath, erec 1836. Note that some Darlaston entries may be included in the registers of Springhead, Wednesdbury (Wes).

DARLASTON, Blockall. A non-conformist chapel was registered in 1830 but no denomination was given.

DEADMAN'S GREEN (Ind). See under CHECKLEY.

DILHORNE All Saints (L) (1510). OR C 1559-1846, M 1559-1960, B 1559-1933 (SRO). BT 1663-1862 (gaps 1753, 1840) (LJRO). COP CMB 1561-1812 Ms (WSL), Extr C 1662-1862, M 1662-1843 (IGI), M 1561-1837 (SMI).

DILHORNE (Wes), erec before 1820.

DILHORNE (Wes), erec 1827.

DILHORNE (Wes), Blythe Marsh Chapel, erec 1821.

DRAYCOTT-IN-THE-MOORS St Margaret (L) (539). OR CMB 1669-72, CM 1678-1812, M 1813-37, B 1678-1720, 1729, 1747-1812 (SRO), CB 1813+ (Inc). BT 1676-1868 (gaps 1679-82, 1732-35, 1744-47, 1766-70, 1854) (LJRO). COP CMB 1780-1841 Ms (WSL), Extr C 1676-1868, M 1813-57 (IGI).

DRAYCOTT-IN-THE-MOORS (RC), St Mary, Cresswell, reg 1791. OR C 1780+ M 1837+ (Inc). COP C 1780-1819 ptd (SPRS), Extr C 1780-1819 (IGI).

DRAYTON BASSETT St Peter (L) (459). OR C 1559-1943, M 1559-1836, B 1559-1899, Banns 1823-1940 (SRO). BT 1664-1881 (gaps 1741-44, 1766-70, 1786-91, M 1795-99, 1800, 1854-55, 1878) (LJRO). COP CMB 1559-1722 Ms (WSL), Extr C 1664-1875, M 1664-1881 (IGI), M 1559-1722 (SMI).

DRAYTON-IN-HALES St Mary, Chapelry, erec 1833. Covers that part of the parish of Market Drayton, Shropshire, lying in Staffordshire, comprising the three townships of Almington, Bloore-in-Tyrley and Hales (L).

DUDLEY PORT. See under TIPTON.

DUNSTON St Leonard. Chapelry to Penkridge becoming a parish in 1844 (L). Royal Peculiar of Penkridge. OR C 1853-1952 (SRO), early entries should be included in the registers of Penkridge. BT 1854-60 (gap 1856-57) (LJRO).

EASTWOOD VALE (Meth NC). See under STOKE-UPON-TRENT.

EATON CHURCH. See under CHURCH EATON.

ECCLESHALL Holy Trinity (L) (4471). Peculiar of the Prebend of Eccleshall. OR CMB 1573+ (Inc). BT 1659-1881 (gaps 1666-71, 1682, 1699, 1708-09, 1718-1802, M 1802-12, 1824-64, 1871) (LJRO). COP CMB 1573-1618 ptd (SPRS), CMB 1573-1812 Mf (SRO), CMB 1653-1783 Ms (WSL), CMB 1703-83 Ms (LJRO), M 1573-1783 (SMI), M 1573-1618 (CMI), Extr C 1573-1611, 1620-27, 1659-1717, 1802-75, M 1573-1617, 1620-1717, 1819-56 (IGI). See also under CHAPEL CHORLTON, COTES HEATH and CROXTON.

ECCLESHALL (Ind), f 1822. OR ZC 1822-36 (PRO). COP ZC 1822-36 Mf (SRO), Extr C 1822-36 (IGI).

EDINGALE Holy Trinity. Originally a parochial chapelry to Croxall. Peculiar of the Prebend of Alrewas and Weeford (L) (177). OR C 1575-1695, 1813-1922, M 1575-1695, 1754-1832, B 1575-1812, Banns 1653-59, 1754-1812 (SRO), M 1833+ B 1812+ (Inc). No OR are known for CB 1696-1812, M 1696-1753. BT 1669-1870 (gaps 1669-84, 1735-38, 1765-68) (LJRO). COP Extr C 1669-1810, 1813-70, M 1669-1810, 1813-45 (IGI).

ELFORD St Peter, formerly St Swithin (L) (483). OR C 1558-1872, M 1558-1966, B 1558-1907 (SRO). BT 1633-1864 (gaps 1666-71, 1673-76, 1693-98, 1756-57, 1857-58) (LJRO). COP CMB 1558-1754, M 1754-1812 Ms (WSL), Extr C 1663-1870, M 1663-1847 (IGI).

ELKSTONE, Upper and Lower Elkstone, St John the Baptist, Chapelry to Alstonfield (L) Lic 1785. OR CB 1791+ (Inc). BT 1786-1857 (gaps 1796-99, 1806-08, No marriages). Note C 1851 and B 1851-52 listed under Warslow. BT's also contain some Warslow entries. COP Extr C 1791-1857 (IGI).

ELLASTONE St Peter (L) (1344). OR C 1538-1922, M 1538-1767, 1780-1837, B 1538-1910 (SRO). BT 1661-1869 (gaps 1673-79, 1791-95) (LJRO). COP CMB 1538-1812(I) ptd (SPRS), M 1538-1812 (SMI, CMI), Extr C 1538-1849, M 1538-1848 (IGI).

ELLASTONE (Prim), Ramsor Circuit, f 1810. OR ZC 1826-37 (PRO). COP ZC 1826-37 Mf(SRO), Extr C 1826-37 (IGI).

ELLASTONE (Prim), reg 1837.

ELLASTONE, Stanton. A nonconformist chapel was registered in 1927 but no denomination was given.

ELLENHALL St Michael (L) (286). OR C 1599+ M 1563+ B 1539+ (Inc). BT 1673-1866 (gaps 1705-07, 1854-60, MB 1884-86) (LJRO). COP C 1599-1812, M 1563-1812, B 1539-1812(I) ptd (SPRS), CMB 1653-1836 Ms (WSL), M 1563-1812 (SMI, CMI), Extr C 1599-1875, M 1563-1630, 1644-48, 1675-1835 (IGI).

ELSTON. See under ELKSTONE.

ENDON St Luke (L), Erec 1730. Also called Endon with Stanley. Chapelry to Leek. OR CB 1730+ M 1730-80 (no later marriages) (Inc). BT 1805-62 (no marriages) (LJRO). Pre 1747 Leek BT's contain Endon entries. Post 1812 BT's are listed under Leek, Chapelry of Endon. COP C 1731-1833, M 1733-46, B 1731-44 Ms (WSL), Extr C 1805-62 (IGI).

ENDON (Prim), erec 1832.

ENDON (Wes), erec 1835.

ENFIELD. See under ENVILLE.

ENVILLE St Mary, formerly Enfield. (L) (766). OR C 1627-1858, M 1627-1858, B 1627-1866, Banns 1824-97, few entries 1686-89 (SRO), Certificates of death 1844-77 (SRO). BT 1660-1874 (gaps 1708-11, 1732-35, 1767-69, 1801-04) (LJRO).

ESSINGTON (Wes). See under BUSHBURY.

ETRURIA. See under SHELTON.

ETTINGSHALL Holy Trinity, Chapelry to Sedgley becoming a parish in 1841, erec 1834 (L). OR 1873-1922 (SRO). BT 1837-57 (LJRO). COP C (BT) 1835-56 (IGI).

ETTINGSHALL (Wes), Ettingshall Lane, Hall Lane, George St., New St. OR C 1825-79, M 1900+ (Inc). See also BILSTON, Swan Bank, Oxford Street (Wes).

ETTINGSHALL (Wes), Lanesfield Chapel, erec 1835. OR 1850-1929 (Bilston Meth Ch).

FAIRWELL St Bartholomew (L) (200). Peculiar of the Dean and Chapter of Lichfield. OR C 1693-1954, M 1693-1971, B 1693-1812, Banns 1824-1946, Note that 1744-56 has been torn out of registers, (SRO), B 1812+ (Inc). BT 1666-1867 (gaps 1672-78, 1687-95, 1707-08, 1732-35, 1744-56, 1767-71, 1786-91, 1853) (LJRO). COP Extr C 1663-1744, 1756-1867, M 1663-65, 1676-1743, 1755-1862 (IGI).

FALLINGS HEATH (Wes). See under DARLASTON.

FAREWELL. See under FAIRWELL.

FAWFIELD HEAD (Prim), Hulme End. See under ALSTONFIELD.

FAZELEY St Paul, chapelry to Tamworth becoming a parish in 1842, erec 1810 (L). No burial ground. OR CM 1816+ (Inc). BT 1843-67 (LJRO), for earlier BT's see under Tamworth. COP Extr C 1842-67 (IGI).

FAZELEY (Ind), Lady Meadow, reg 1826.

FAZELEY (Wes), erec 1823.

FENTON. See under STOKE-ON-TRENT.

FLASH. See under QUARNFORD.

FORTON All Saints (L) (922). OR CMB 1558+ (Inc). BT 1660-1868 (gaps 1665-73, 1679-82, 1693, 1718-22, 1763-69, 1855, 1858-62) (LJRO). COP CB 1558-1754, M 1558-1812(I) (WSL), M 1558-1812 (SMI), Extr C 1660-1868, M 1660-1837 (IGI).

FORTON. A non-conformist chapel was registered in 1836 but no denomination was given.

FOX EARTH (Meth NC). See under CAVERSWALL.

FOXT (Prim Meth). See under IPSTONES.

FRADLEY (S of F). See under ALREWAS.

FRADSWELL St James alias FRODESWELL, Chapelry to Colwich until 1851 (L). Peculiar of the Prebend of Colwich. OR CMB 1578-1615, 1636-93, 1704-62 (damaged and not available to the public), 1769-1812, C 1813-1914, M 1814-37, B 1813-1978 (SRO). BT 1666-1856 (gaps 1672-78, 1707-08, 1732-35, 1753-56, 1767-71, 1775-76, 1786-91, 1836-47, 1849-53) (LJRO). COP Extr C 1666-1835, 1848-57, M 1666-1835, C 1848-49 (IGI).

FREEHAY (Prim Meth), Heapwood Chapel. See under CHEADLE.

FRODESWELL St James. See under FRADSWELL.

FULFORD St Nicholas, Chapelry to Stone (L). OR CMB 1827+ (Inc). BT 1800-66, listed with Stone 1701-1808 and some post 1856 (gaps B 1856, 1858-62, some M 1837-63) (LJRO). COP Mf of Stone includes Fulford (SRO), Extr CM 1813-63 (IGI).

FULFORD (Meth NC), Zion Chapel, f 1805.

FARSHALL GREEN (Wes). See under MILWICH.

GAYTON St Peter (L) (296). OR C 1593-1927, M 1593-1836, B 1593-1812 (gaps 1695-1704, Banns 1755-1823 (SRO), B 1813+ (Inc). BT 1661-1856 (gaps 1759-69) (LJRO).

GENTLESHAW Christ Church, Chapelry to Longdon becoming a parish in 1840, erec 1837 (L). OR CMB 1837+ (Inc). BT 1837-74 (gaps 1845, 1853, 1855) (LJRO).

GENTLESHAW (Ind), erec 1824.

GNOSALL St Lawrence (L) (3358). Peculiar of the Manor of Gnosall. OR C 1572-1902, M 1572-1913, B 1572-1848 (entries CMB 1640-61 incomplete), Banns 1823-52 (SRO). BT 1687-1836 (gaps 1693-95, 1700-01, 1705-08, 1742-43, 1748-54, 1758-99, only fragments of 1745-47 exist) (LJRO). COP CB 1572-1699, M 1572-1785 ptd(SPRS), M 1572-1785 (SMI, CMI), Extr C 1572-1699, 1702-04, 1739-57, 1800-36, M 1702-04, 1739-57, 1800-36 (IGI).

GNOSALL (Ind), Bromstead Heath, reg 1795.

GNOSALL (Ind), Ebenezer Chapel, Coton End, erec 1823.

GNOSAL (Prim Meth), erec before 1800.

GOLDEN HILL (Wes). See under WOLSTANTON.

GORNAL LOWER St James, Chapelry to Sedgley, erec 1823 (L). Peculiar of the Manor of Sedgley. OR C 1823-99, M 1838-1911, B 1823-1905 (DPL). BT 1823-47 (LJRO). COP Extr C 1823-47 (IGI).

GORNAL UPPER (Ind), Ruiton Chapel, f 1778. This was probably initially a Lady Hunt Conn chapel. OR ZC 1778-1827, 1816-1837, B 1792-1837 (PRO). COP C 1778-98, ZC 1810-27 Mf (SRO), C 1777-1877, 1837-83 Extr, M 1837-83, B 1792-1837 Ms (DPL), CB 1792-1837 (I) Ms (WSL), CB 1778-1837 Ms (WoPL), Extr C 1778-1837 (IGI).

GORNAL (Lady Hunt Conn), erec 1777. See under GORNAL UPPER.

GORNAL WOOD (Meth NC), Zoar Chapel, Sedgley, erec 1837.

GORNWAL WOOD (Wes), Himley Road, erec 1826.

GORNAL UPPER (Wes), erec 1832.

GOSPEL ASH (Wes). See under BOBBINGTON.

GOSPEL OAK (Wes). See under TIPTON.

GRATWICH St Mary (L) (116). OR M 1755-1834 (SRO), C 1813+ M 1834+ B 1813+ (Inc). BT 1680-1869 (gaps 1686-93, 1767-69, 1853-63), 1791-95 included in terriers (LJRO). COP Extr C 1680-1864, M 1680-1834 (IGI).

GREAT BARR St Margaret, Chapelry to Aldridge (L). OR CMB 1654+ (Inc). BT 1664-1870 (gaps 1810-12, 1853-63) (LJRO). COP CMB 1654-1749 Ms (WSL), CMB 1654-1749(I) (SG), Extr C 1660-1809, 1813-52, 1864-70, M 1660-85, 1698-1763, 1791-1809 (IGI).

GREAT BRIDGE (Wes). See under TIPTON

GREAT HAYWOOD (RC). See under TIXAL.

GREAT WYRLEY. See under NORTON CANES.

GREETS GREEN. See under WEST BROMWICH.

GRINDON All Saints (L) (431). OR C 1697-1880, M 1697-1837, B 1697-1936, Banns 1755-1958 (SRO), (Note CMB 1697-1782 include some entries for Onecote). BT 1679-1852 (gaps 1694, 1762-66, 1770-73, 1847-49, M 1771-91) (LJRO). COP Extr CM 1679-1852 (IGI).

HALMEREND. See under AUDLEY.

HAMMERWICH St John (L) (218). Peculiar of the Dean of Lichfield. OR CMB 1720+ (Inc). BT 1727-1864 (gaps 1735-38, 1743-44)(LJRO). COP Extr C 1727-44, 1774-1865, M 1727-44, 1777-1810, 1817-34 (IGI).

HAMSTALL RIDWARE. See under RIDWARE.

HANBURY St Werburga (L) (2160). OR C 1574-1864, M 1574-1837, B 1574-1881, Banns 1823-1964 (SRO). BT 1661-1861 (gaps 1735-37, 1857-61) (LJRO). COP CB 1574-1812, M 1574-1744, 1770-1803, Banns 1770-1802 Ms (WSL), CB 1574-1812, M 1574-1744, 1770-1803, Banns 1770-1802 Mf of Ms (HPL), Extr C 1661-1809, 1813-56, M 1661-1836 (IGI), M 1574-1812 (SMI). See also under MARCHINGTON and NEWBOROUGH.

HANBURY (Wes), erec 1828.

HANDFORD. See under HANFORD.

HANDSACRE. See under ARMITAGE.

HANDSWORTH St Mary (L) (4944), formerly Staffs. but since 1911 in Warcs. and in the Birmingham Diocese since 1905. OR CMB 1558+ (Inc). BT 1660-1809 (gaps 1735-38) (BRL), 1805-89 (gaps CB 1866-89) (LJRO). COP CMB 1558-1605 (Joseph Hill's notebooks BRL), CMB 1660-1736 Ms (BRL), M 1830-37 (GBMI), Extr C 1805-65, M 1810-37 (IGI). See also under PERRY BARR.

HANDSWORTH (RC), Oscott, erec 1778. Variously referred to as Oscott, nowadays as Old Oscott and Maryvale. OR C 1794+ M 1822+ (Inc).

HANDSWORTH (Ind), Union Chapel, f 1788. Originally a chapel of the Lady Hunt.Conn, closing in 1805 for two years and re-opening as Ind. OR ZC 1788-1837, B 1827-37 (PRO). COP ZC 1788-1827 Mf (SRO), Extr C 1788-1837 (IGI).

HANDWORTH (Ind), Newton, erec 1803.

HANDSWORTH (Lady Hunt Conn), erec 1789. Closed about 1805 and later re-opening as an Independent chapel. See under HANDSWORTH (Ind).

HANFORD, Chapel to Trentham becoming a parish in 1832, erec 1828 (L). OR ?CMB 1828+ (Inc). BT 1828-68 (gaps 1840-50) (LJRO). COP Extr C 1828-58 (IGI).

HANFORD (Meth NC), reg 1812.

HANLEY St John th Baptist, erec 1737 (L). Chapelry to Stoke-on-Trent until it became a parish in 1857. OR C 1789-1803, 1842+ M 1837+ B 1827+ (Inc), original regs. presumed destoryed during 1842 riots, dating from at least 1754 and c1803-42. BT CB 1744-47 (with Stoke-on-Trent BT's,) 1791-1835 (LJRO). COP CB 1743-46, C 1748 ptd with Stoke-on-Trent (SPRS), C 1789-1803(I) ptd (BMSGH), C 1789-1803, 1842-81, M 1837-63 (in format of Boyd's), B 1827-56 Ms (HPL), Extr C 1789-1803, 1805-35, M 1816-35 (IGI). See also under SHELTON.

HANLEY (Part Bapt), f 1789. Chapels at various times in Slacks Lane, Miles Bank and New Street. Church closed during perod 1804 to 1820. Burial ground at New Street opened 1821. OR None known before 1879.

HANLEY (Ind), Tabernacle, High Street, f 1784, previously Lady Hunt Conn.
OR ZC 1786-1837 (PRO). COP ZC 1786-1806, 1816-37 Mf (HPL), Extr
C 1784-1837 (IGI).

HANLEY (Lady Hunt Conn), Tabernacle, erec 1784, later became Independent.
See under Hanley (Ind).

HANLEY (Meth NC), Tabernacle, High Street, reg 1819. OR For Hanley Circuit
see under SHELTON.

HANLEY UPPER (Meth NC), Providence Chapel, f 1819. OR For Hanley Circuit
see under SHELTON.

HANLEY (Prim Method), Stafford Road, reg 1824.

HANLEY (Wes), Old Hall Street, corner of Claverly street, f before 1800.
Some Hanley baptisms are included in the register of Burslem, Swan Bank
(Wes). OR ZC 1818-37 (PRO). COP ZC 1818-36 Mf (HPL), Extr C 1818-
37 (IGI).

HANLEY (Wes Meth Assoc), Old House, Northwood, erec before 1800.

HARBORNE St Peter (L) (4227), formerly in Staffordshire and in Warwickshire
from 1891. Peculiar of the Dean and Chapter of Lichfield. OR C 1538-
1955, M 1538-1967, B 1538-1954 (gaps 1647-53), C 1673-74, M 1673-76,
B 1673-75), Banns 1797-1840 (BRL). BT 1660-1856 (gaps 1667-71, 1838-
49, 1852-55) (LJRO). COP C 1538-1813, M 1538-1807, B 1538-1812 (gaps
CMB 1647-53) (BRL), M 1806-12 (surnames only, by year) Ms (LJRO), M
1823-37 (Boyd), Extr C 1813-37, 1850-69, M 1813-37 (IGI). See also under
SMETHWICK.

HARLASTON St Matthew, Chapelry to Clifton Campville until 1845. OR CMB
1693+ (Inc). Account of an earlier register can be found in the Court of
the Bishop of Lichfield. BT 1679-1870 (gaps 1747-62, 1766-70, 1838, 1869)
(LJRO). For 1837 see under Clifton Campville. COP Extr C 1665-1870
(IGI).

HARPSFIELD (Meth NC). See under STOKE-ON-TRENT.

HARRISEAHEAD (Wes). See under WOLSTANTON.

HARTS HILL (Ind). See under BRIERLEY HILL.

HARTSHILL COMMON. See under STOKE-ON-TRENT.

HAUGHTON St Giles (L) (490). OR C 1570-1865, M 1570-1835, B 1570-1907
(gap CMB 1705-11), Banns 1824-1903 (SRO), M 1835+ (Inc). BT 1659-1878
(gaps 1856, 1861, 1875) (LJRO). COP CMB 1570-1812(I) ptd (SPRS), M
1570-1812 (SMI, CMI), Extr C 1570-1685, 1696-1706, 1711-1876, M 1570-
1753, 1813-43 (IGI).

HEATON (Wes). See under LEEK.

HIGHERLAND (Prim Meth). See under NEWCASTLE-UNDER-LYME.

HIGH OFFLEY St Mary the Virgin (L) (827). Peculiar of the Prebend of Offley
and Flixton. OR CMB 1689+ (Inc). BT 1659-1875 (gaps 1662-71, 1678-
81, 1692-96, 1721-27) (LJRO). COP CMB 1659-1812(I) ptd (BMSGH), CMB
1660-1812 (with Church Eaton) Ms (WSL), M 1659-1812 (SMI), M 1813-36
(IGI).

HILDERSTONE Christ Church. (L). CHapelry to Stone becoming a parish in
1840, erec 1832. OR 1830+ (Inc). BT 1833-71 (entries also under STONE)
(LJRO). COP Extr C 1833-68 (IGI).

HILDERSTONE (Wes), erec 1822.

HILL CHORLTON (Wes). See under CHAPEL CHORLTON.

40

HILL RIDWARE. See under RIDWARE MAVESYN.

HILL TOP. See under WEST BROMWICH.

HIMLEY St Michael (L) (421). OR CMB 1665+ (Inc). BT 1664-1885 (gaps 1666-67, 1674-75, 1685-92, 1731, 1756-61, 1763-65) (LJRO). COP CMB 1665-1812 ptd (SPRS), M 1665-1837 (SMI), Extr C 1665-1875, M 1671-1837 (IGI).

HINTS St Bartholomew (L) (225). Peculiar of the Prebend of Handsacre and Armitage. OR CB 1559-1812, M 1559-1754 (SRO), CB 1812+ M 1754+ (Inc). BT 1659-1828 (gaps 1792-95) (LJRO). COP CMB 1558-1812(I) ptd (SPRS), M 1558-1812 (SMI, CMI), Extr CM 1558-1828 (IGI).

HOLLINGSCLOUGH (Wes). See under ALSTONFIELD.

HOLLINGTON HEATH (Prim Meth). See under CHECKLEY.

HOLY CROSS (Bapt). See under CLENT.

HOOKGATE (Prim Meth). See under ASHLEY.

HORSLEY FIELDS (Meth NC). See under WOLVERHAMPTON.

HORTON St Michael (L) (970). OR CMB 1653-84, 1725+ (Inc). BT 1673-1872 (gaps 1674, 1676, 1686-92, 1698-1701, 1723, 1771-72, 1853, 1857, 1867, 1869) (LJRO). COP Extr C 1673-1870, M 1678-1836 (IGI).

HORTON Gate House Bank. A non-conformist chapel was registered in 1816 but no denomination was given.

HULME END (Prim Meth). See under ALSTONFIELD.

ILAM Holy Cross (L) (210). OR C 1651-1813, M 1651-1836, B 1651-1812, Banns 1790-1809 (SRO), CB 1813+ (Inc). BT 1661-1868 (gaps 1705-10, 1755-58, 1762-66, 1861) (LJRO). COP Extr C 1661-1868, M 1661-1836 (IGI).

INGESTRE St Mary (L) (116). OR CMB 1691+ (Inc). BT 1676-1839 (LJRO). COP Extr C 1676-1839, M 1676-1839 (IGI).

IPSTONES St Leonard (L) (1384). OR C 1561-1934, M 1561-1948, B 1561-1942 (gaps CMB 1716-26, C 1868-82, M 1783), Banns 1891-1923 (SRO). BT 1673-1857 (gaps 1677-78, 1763-65, 1821, CM 1849-57, B 1852) (LJRO). COP CMB 1561-1716 Ms (SG), M 1561-1716 (SMI), Extr C 1673-1847, M 1673-1837 (IGI).

IPSTONES (S of F), Mordige, f 1672. Part of Leek MM.

IPSTONES (S of F), Whitehough, f 1672. Member of Leek MM.

IPSTONES (Prim Meth), erec 1820. OR M 1930-46 (SRO).

IPSTONES (Prim Meth), Foxt, erec 1812.

KEELE St John the Baptist (L) (1130). OR CM 1540-1980, B 1540-1904, Banns 1823-1980 (SRO). BT 1668-1869 (gaps 1675-79), 1684-90, 1766-70, 1856, 1866) (LJRO). COP C 1540-1700, M 1540-1812 ptd (SPRS), CB 1540-1812, M 1543-1812 Ms (WSL), CB 1540-1812, M 1543-1812 Mf of Ms (HPL), M 1540-1812 (SMI, CMI), Extr C 1540-1870, M 1543-1870 (IGI).

KEELE (Meth NC), Bethel Chapel, erec before 1800.

KEELE (Wes), erec 1835.

KIDSGROVE erec 1837 as a private chapel. OR 1839+ (Inc).

KINFARE. See under KINVER.

KING'S BROMLEY All Saints (L) (629). Also called Bromley Regis. Peculiar of the Prebend of Alrewas and Weeford. OR CMB 1673+ (Inc). BT 1632-1869 (gaps 1632-63, 1666-68, 1672-75, 1678-84, 1710-11). COP Extr C 1632-1869, M 1632-1837 (IGI).

KING'S BROMLEY (Prim Meth), erec 1836.

KINGSLEY St Werburgh (L) (1416). OR C 1561-1938, M 1561-1931, B 1561-
1945, Banns 1754-82, 1813-18, 1824-39 (SRO). BT 1673-1854 (gaps 1679-
82, 1687-89, M 1773-76) (LJRO). COP CMB 1561-1754, CB 1754-95 ptd
(SPRS), M 1561-1754 (SMI, CMI), Extr C 1561-1857, M 1561-1754, 1813-
37 (IGI).

KINGSLEY (Prim Meth), erec 1834.

KINGSLEY (Prim Meth), Whiston, erec 1816.

KINGSLEY (Wes), erec 1812.

KINGSLEY (Wes), Whiston, erec 1836.

KINGSTONE St John (L) (368). OR C 1813-75, M 1755-1837, B 1813-1938
(SRO). BT 1679-1868 (gaps 1682-85, 1701-05, 1735-38, 1791-94, 1856-64)
(LJRO). COP Extr C 1682-1868, M 1679-1837 (IGI).

KINGSWINFORD St Mary (L) (15156). This was the Parish Church of Kingswinford
until 1831 when it became a Chapelry to the new Parish Church of Kingswinford,
namely Holy Trinity at Wordsley. In 1846 it became a parish again in
its own right. OR C 1832-1914, M 1837-1910, B 1832-1944 (DPL). Note
the registers for 1603-1832 are listed under WORDSLEY Holy Trinity
having been trasnferred there in 1832 and the entries being continued
in the same books, Banns 1754-1811 (held under WORDSLEY Holy Trinity)(DPL).
BT 1666-1857 (gaps 1693-97, 1709-13, 1841-44) (LJRO). COP Extr CMB
1603-1811 (SRO), Extr C 1718-76, 1800-31, 1834-48, M 1718-1837 (IGI),
CMB 1603-1812, C 1813-1904, M 1812-76, B 1813-37, Banns 1754-1811
Mf (SRO). See also BRIERLEY HILL and WORDSLEY.

KINGSWINFORD (Pres), Pensnett Chase, reg 1704. This group later formed
the Park Lane Presbyterian Chapel, Cradley, Worcestershire in 1796.
OR C 1736-1837 B 1761-1826 (few entries) (PRO classed as Park Lane
Pres. Church, Cradley, Worcs.). COP C 1736-1836 B 1761-1826 ptd (Park
Lane Pres. Church, Cradley, Worcs., BMSGH).

KINGSWINFORD (Meth NC), Amblecot, Brettell Lane, f c.1836. Took over
a chapel previously occupied by the Wesleyans in about 1836.

KINGSWINFORD (Meth NC), Cradley Forge, erec before 1800.

KINGSWINFORD (Meth NC), St James Chapel, Pensnett, erec 1837. OR C
1886-1939 (Inc).

KINGSWINFORD (Prim Meth), erec 1833. Many Kingswinford entries are contained
in the Circuit Register. See also BRIERLEY HILL, Round Oak.

KINGSWINFORD (Prim Meth), Pensnett, Shut End, erec 1832. COP C 1845-
87 (Ms author).

KINGSWINFORD (Wes), Amblecote, Brettell Lane, erec 1831. Chapel in Brettell
Lane sold to Meth NC c.1836. The Wesleyans built a new Centenary Chapel
in the High Street in 1839.

KINGSWINFORD (Wes), Pensnett, erec 1835. OR C 1851-1965 (Inc St James,
Pensnett).

KINGSWINFORD, Buckpool. A non-conformist chapel was registered in 1799
but no denomination was given.

KINVER St Peter (L) (1831). Also called Kinfare. OR C 1560-1904, M 1560-
1915, B 1560-1907 (gap 1650-52), Banns 1823-97 (SRO). BT 1655-1880
(gaps 1755-58, 1762-73, 1854-55) (LJRO). COP C 1560-1775, M 1560-1804,
B 1560-1756 Ms (WSL, SG), CMB 1718-1804 Ms (WoPL), Extr C 1655-1762,
1782-1875, M 1655-1838 (IGI).

KINVER (Bapt), erec 1814. Chapel taken over by Curate of Kinver in 1827 for Sunday School. Later taken over by Prim Meths and then by Wes Meths in 1839/40.

KINVER (Prim Meth). Took over chapel previously belonging to the Baptists in about 1830 until about 1839.

KNIGHTON. See under MUCKLESTONE.

KNOWLE END (Wes). See under AUDLEY.

KNUTTON (S of F). See under WOLSTANTON.

KNUTTON HEATH (Wes). See under WOLSTANTON.

LADY MEADOW (Ind). See under FAZELEY.

LANE END. Longton was usually called Lane End until the end of the nineteenth century. See under LONGTON.

LAPLEY All Saint (L) (1042). Entries from Wheaton Aston are included with Lapley. OR C 1538-1971, M 1538-1969, B 1538-1938 (gap 1810-12), Banns 1754-1809, 1823-80 (SRO). BT 1664-1878 (gaps 1665-67, 1668-73, 1685-93, 1711-14, 1774-75, 1787-90, 1853-55, 1858-60, 1876)(LJRO). COP CMB 1538-1756 Ms (WSL), Extr C 1664-1877, M 1738-1812, 1814-35 (IGI). M 1538-1756 (SMI). See also under WHEATON ASTON.

LEEK St Edward the Confessor (L) (10,780). OR C 1634-1849, M 1634-1837, B 1634-1791 (gap 1698-1700), Banns 1754-56 (SRO), B 1791+ (Inc). BT 1662-1853 (gaps 1666-73, 1677, 1756-57, 1767-70, 1854-63) BT's also contain some Endon entries (LJRO). COP CMB 1634-95 ptd (SPRS), C 1695-98, 1700-1812, M 1695-98, 1700-54, B 1678-1707 Ms (WSL), C 1695-1812, M 1695-98, 1700-80, 1790-1812, B 1678-1812 Mf of Ms (HPL, NPL, SG), M 1634-95 (CMI, SMI), Extr C 1634-1853, M 1562-1747 (IGI). See also under ENDON MEERBROOK, ONECOTE and 'RUSHTON SPENCER.

LEEK (RC), St Mary, Fountain Street, erec 1829. OR C 1830+ M 1844+ (Inc).

LEEK (S of F), Overtons Bank. Leek MM amalgamated with Stafford MM in 1783. OR MM Z 1833-37, M 1831-37, B 1831-37 (PRO), Minute Book 1705-37 (SRO), Minute Book of Women's MM 1708-17 (SRO), Record of Suffering 1655-1792, Notices of Intended Marriages 1703-55, Certs of Removal to & from Leek MM 1709-91 (SRO), Discussions, denials, disownments, testimonies, etc. mainly Leek with a few Stafford MM 1718-95, Members 1703-95 (SRO).

LEEK (Part Bapt), Lower End, reg 1815.

LEEK (Ind), Derby Street, f 1782. OR ZC 1787-1837, DB 1797-1837 (PRO). COP C 1785-1832, B 1797-1836 Mf (SRO), Extr C 1785-1837 (IGI).

LEEK (Ind), Union Street, erec 1833. OR C 1831-37 (PRO). COP C 1830-37 (SRO), C 1829-37 (IGI).

LEEK (Prim Meth), Fountain Street, erec 1836. OR M 1925-48 (SRO).

LEEK (Wes), Mount Pleasant, f 1786. OR ZC 1808-37 (PRO), C 1837-69, M 1912-77, Burial ground accounts 1837-1909 (SRO). COP ZC 1808-37 Mf (SRO), C 1808-37 (IGI).

LEEK (Wes), West Street Sunday School. OR Admission registers 1804-44, Minutes, Accounts 1802-1938, Sunday School Book 1799-1922 (SRO).

LEEK (Wes), Brunswick Chapel, Ballhaye Street, erec 1820. OR C 1861-93 (SRO).

LEEK (Wes), Heaton, erec 1816.

LEEK (Wes), Leekfrith, erec 1811.

LEEKFRITH (Wes). See above.

LEIGH All Saints (L) (1038). OR C 1541-1872, M 1541-1842, B 1541-1860, Banns 1754-1809, 1824-1901 (SRO). BT 1660-1854 (gaps 1664-70, 1679, 1767-69) (LJRO). COP CMB 1541-1704 Ms, 1704-67 Mf (SRO), CMB 1541-1701 Ms (Inc), Extr C 1660-1854, M 1813-41 (IGI).

LEIGH (Prim Meth), Moor High Heath, erec 1815.

LICHFIELD Cathedral (247). Peculiar of the Dean of Lichfield. OR CMB 1660+ (Inc). BT 1744-1892 (gaps M 1755-66, B 1888-92) (LJRO). COP CB 1660-1774, M 1665-1754 ptd (SPRS), M 1660-1754 (SMI, CMI), Extr C 1660-1875, M 1665-1879 (IGI).

LICHFIELD St Chad (At Stowe-by-Lichfield) (L) (2243). Peculiar of the Dean of Lichfield. OR C 1635-1903, M 1635-1912, B 1635-1925, Banns 1754-74 (LJRO). BT 1659-1892 (gaps 1660-61, M 1666-69, 1692-94, 1698-1702) (LJRO). COP Extr C 1659-1877, M 1659-1812, 1814-37 (IGI).

LICHFIELD St Mary (L) (4377). Peculiar of the Dean of Lichfield. OR C 1566-1917, M 1566-1947, B 1566-1891, Banns 1754-92, 1823-1954 (LJRO). Note that St Mary's has no churchyard. From 1581 the place of burial is given and is normally St Chad's or St Michael's, although in later years it is more likely to be St Michael's. BT 1659-1868 (gaps 1666-72, 1675-78) (LJRO). COP CMB 1566-76 Ms (WSL), Extr CMB 1640-1810 (WSL), Extr C 1659-1868, M 1659-1837 (IGI). See also under BURNTWOOD.

LICHFIELD St Michael (L) (2708). Peculiar of the Dean of Lichfield. OR C 1574-1933, M 1574-1945, B 1574-1940, Banns 1754-62 (LJRO). BT 1663-1868 (gaps 1666-91, 1697-1701, 1774-77, 1792-05, 1850, 1863) (LJRO). COP CMB 1574-1741, Extr CMB 1574-1783 (WSL), Extr C 1663-66, 1691-1868, M 1663-66, 1690-1837 (IGI).

LICHFIELD Christ Church District Chapelry, in the parish of St Michael, lic 1820. BT 1848-74 (LJRO).

LICHFIELD Chapel of the Hospital of St John the Baptist, erec before 1800.

LICHFIELD (RC), Holy Cross Chapel, St John Street. OR C 1788+ M 1803+ Confms 1806+ (Inc). COP C 1788+ M 1803+ Ms (DA).

LICHFIELD (S of F). From 1816 to 1929 in the Birmingham MM. OR Registers for the Birmingham MM are at the Friends Meeting House, Bull Street, Birmingham.

LICHFIELD (Ind), Wade Street formerly Sandford Street, f 1790 in Sandford Street but was closed between 1796 and 1802. OR ZC 1801-37 (PRO). COP C 1801-1837 Mf (SRO), C 1801-37 (IGI).

LICHFIELD (Meth NC), Ebenezer Chapel, Queen Street, erec 1833.

LICHFIELD (Wes), Wade Street, f 1815. OR ZC 1815-37 (PRO). COP C 1815-37 Mf (SRO), C 1815-92 Ms (Inc), C 1815-37 (IGI).

LIGHTWOOD (Meth NC). See under STONE.

LITTLE LONDON (Part Bapt). See under WILLENHALL.

LONGDON St James (L) (1147). Peculiar of the Prebend of Longdon. OR C 1687-1872, M 1687-1841, B 1687-1908 (SRO). BT 1663-1869 (gaps 1666-70, 1672-73, 1680-84, 1689-92, 1717-21, 1730-32) (LJRO). COP CMB(BT) 1663-87 Ms (WSL), CMB 1663-1812 Ms (WSL), Extr C 1663-1868, M 1663-1851 (IGI). See also under BRERETON and GENTLESHAW.

LONGDON (Ind), previously Presbyterian, f 1672.

LONGDON (Wes), erec 1830.

LONGNOR St Bartholomew (L), Chapelry to Alstonfield. OR CB 1691-1789, M
1702-54, in one volume in poor condition, says previous volume (not now
extant) was worse, CB 1789-1812, M 1754-86, 1812, Banns 1754-68, 1786,
1811-55 (SRO), CMB 1812+ (Inc). BT 1690-1853 (gaps 1693-1708, 1705-08,
1763-69, 1786-95, 1820, 1824, 1847-48) (LJRO).

LONGNOR (S of F), reg 1723.

LONGNOR (Wes), f before 1800.

LONGPORT (Wes). See under BURSLEM.

LONGTON St John (L), erec 1763. Longton was usually called Lane End until the
end of the nineteenth century becoming a parish in 1839 having been
previously a Chapelry to Stoke-on-Trent. OR C 1764-1976, M 1866-1975, B
1764-1975 (SRO). BT 1764-1868 (gaps 1773-94, 1854-55), No Marriages
(LJRO), 1773-90 (WSL). COP CB 1764-90 Ms (WSL), Extr C 1764-73, 1800-09,
1828-68 (IGI).

LONGTON St James, High Street, Chapelry to Longton St John, erec 1834 (L). OR
C 1834-1909, M 1837-1913, B 1834-1915 (SRO). BT 1834-39 (filed with Lane
End) (LJRO). COP C 1834-39 (IGI).

LONGTON (RC), St Gregory, erec 1818. OR C 1822+ M 1869+ (Inc).

LONGTON (Ind), Caroline Street (Lane End), f 181. OR ZC 1819-37 (PRO). COP ZC
1818-37 Mf (HPL), C 1819-37 (IGI).

MADELEY All Saints (L) (1190). OR C 1678-1902, M 1678-1928, B 1678-1938,
Banns 1823-1941 (SRO). BT 1682-1853 (gaps 1776-82, 1809-12) (LJRO). COP
CMB 1567-1775, M 1775-1812 ptd (SPRS), CB 1775-1812 ptd (BMSGH), M 1567-
1812 (SMI, CMI), Extr C 1567-1775, M 1776-1808, 1813-53 (IGI).

MADELEY (S of F), reg 1731.

MADELEY (S of F), Stonylow, reg 1730.

MADELEY (Wes), erec 1831.

MAER St Peter (L) (505). OR CMB 1558-65, 1569-1668, 1680-92, 1694-1809, C1810-
74, M 1810-37, Banns 1823-1964 (SRO), B 1813 + (Inc). BT 1674-1878 (gaps
1693-98, 1773-76, 1786-90. 1853, 1856); entries from 1791 to 1795 are
undated; several terriers included in BT's (LJRO). COP CMB 1558-1812 Ms
(WSL), M 1558-1812 (SMI), Extr C 1674-1878, M 1679-1848 (IGI).

MARCHINGTON St Peter (L), Chapelry to Hanbury. OR CMB 1612-70 (gaps 1644-
48) (SRO), CMB 1670+ (Inc). BT 1667-1868 (gaps 1668-75, 1714-15, 1838-40,
1845-58) (LJRO). COP CMB 1609-70, incomplete until CB 1759-1812, M 1774-
1812 Ms (WSL), M 1617-32 (Boyd Misc), Extr C 1813-65, M 1813-44 (IGI).

MARSTON St Leonard (L), Chapelry to Stafford St Mary. No burial ground. OR
CMB 1565-1757 (one mutilated volume 1565-86, 1607-42, 1647-61, odd entries
1662-1716, three loose folios 1718-56) C 1767-1954, M 1841-1955, B 1813-73
(SRO). BT 1661-1862 (gaps 1685-1711, 1723-29, 1748-93, 1854-56) (LJRO).
COP C 1556-1757, MB 1556-1744 (I) Ms (WSL), Extr C 1566-1757, 1794-1854
(IGI).

MARYVALE (RC). See under HANDSWORTH.

MATHFIELD. See under MAYFIELD.

MAVESYN RIDWARE. See under RIDWARE.

MAYERS GREEN (Ind). See under WEST BROMWICH.

MAYFIELD St John the Baptist (L) (729). OR C 1573-1968, M 1573-1952, B 1573-
1846, 1857-99 (gap CMB 1664-73), Banns 1754-88, 1796-97, 1823-90 (SRO). BT
1676-1868 (gaps 1705-08, 1713-18) (LJRO). COP Extr C 1676-1812, 1814-68,
M 1676-1812, 1814-52 (IGI). See also under BUTTERTON.

MAYFIELD. A nonconformist chapel was registered in 1816 but no denomination was given.

MEERBROOK, Chapelry to Leek until 1859. (L). OR C 1738-1925, M 1738-54, B 1738-1812 (SRO), Note that there are no marriages after 1754, B 1812+ (Inc). BT 1791-1863 (gap 1854). COP Extr C 1813-63 (IGI).

MILLDALE (Prim Meth). See under ALSTONFIELD.

MILTON. See under NORTON-IN-THE-MOORS.

MILLWICH All Saints (L) (551). OR C 1573-1855, M 1573-1837, B 1573-1890 (gap 1685-1700) (SRO). BT 1636-1885 (gaps 1639-59, 1711-13, 1826, M 1840-48, 1853-55, 1856-85, 1862, 1864, M 1853-85) (LJRO). COP CMB 1573-1711 ptd (SPRS), M 1573-1711 (SMI, CMI), Extr C 1573-1711, 1714-1875, M 1574-1682, 1695-1711, 1714-1840, 1850-52 (IGI).

MILWICH (Wes), Garshall Green, erec 1835.

MOOR HIGH HEATH (Prim Meth). See under LEIGH.

MORIDGE (S of F). See under IPSTONES.

MOSELEY OLD HALL (RC). See under BUSHBURY.

MOXLEY. See under WEDNESBURY St Bartholomew.

MOXLEY (Wes). See under BILSTON.

MUCKLESTONE St Mary (L) (964). OR CMB 1555+ (Inc). BT 1674-1868 (gaps 1747-51, M 1755-58, M 1786-1800, 1838-39); note that 1755-1758 are damaged; BT's also include Woore Chapelry. (LJRO). COP CMB 1555-1701 ptd (SPRS), CMB 1708-1812 Ms (WSL), M 1555-1808 (SMI), M 1555-1701 (CMI), Extr C 1555-1869, M 1556-1701, 1813-56 (IGI). See also under WOORE.

MUCKLESTONE (Prim Meth), Knighton, erec 1834.

MUCKLESTONE (Wes), Knighton, erec 1834.

NEEDWOOD FOREST Christ Church. This covered land in five parishes - Hanbury, Totenhill, Tutbury, Rolleston and Yoxall. The church dedicated to Christ was erected in 1805 and stood in Rolleston parish. BT 1813-49 (gaps 1830, 1839, 1845-47) (LJRO). COP Extr C 1813-48 (BT) (IGI).

NEWBOROUGH All Saints (L), Chapelry to Hanbury. OR C 1601-1728, 1747-1811, 1813-99, M 1601-99, 1792-1834, Banns 1861-94 (SRO). BT 1660-1844 (gaps 1662, 1667-68, 1708-11, 1747-51, 1767-73, 1810-12, 1839-40; no burials recorded (LJRO). COP CMB 1601-1770 Ms (c/o Miss I.J. Morcom, SRO), Extr C 1660-1809, 1813-44, M 1723-59, 1795-1807, 1814-43 (IGI).

NEWCASTLE-UNDER-LYME St Giles (L) (8192). Chapel to Stoke-on-Trent until 1807. OR C 1563-1918, M 1563-1906, B 1563-1872, (gap CMB 1621-27), Banns 1901-14 (SRO). BT 1662-1864 (gaps 1666-73, 1676-79, 1766-70, 1776-82, 1791-95, 1861-63 (LJRO). COP CMB 1563-1770 ptd (SPRS), CMB 1693-1812 Ms (WSL), Extr CMB 1738-1809 (SG), C 1759-1918, M 1754-1906, B 1769-1872 Mf (NPL), M 1693-1812 (SMI), M 1563-1770 (CMI), Extr C 1563-1620, 1628-1874, M 1563-1770, 1813-42 (IGI).

NEWCASTLE-UNDER-LYME St George (L), Chapelry to St Giles, erec 1828. OR C 1832-1932, M 1837-1946, B 1829-1959 (SRO). BT 1829-74 (gaps C 1829-31) (LJRO). COP C 1832-1932, M 1837-1946, B 1829-1959 Mf (NPL).

NEWCASTLE-UNDER-LYME Holy Trinity (RC), London Road, erec 1832. OR C 1831-35, 1839-59, M 1831 (1), 1842-47 (Inc).

NEWCASTLE-UNDER-LYME (Part Bapt), f between 1814 and 1818, Iron Market 1832-1844, Bridge Street 1844-1854 becoming extinct but restarted in 1867 and Iron Church, erec 1871.

NEWCASTLE-UNDER-LYME (Ind), Marsh Chapel, King Street, f 1777. OR ZC 1777-1836 (PRO). COP C 1777-1836 Mf (NPL), Extr C 1777-1836 (IGI).

NEWCASTLE-UNDER-LYME (Pres), Old Meeting House, f 1690, closed 1804. Later used by Unitarians.

NEWCASTLE-UNDER-LYME (Unit). Took over the premises used by the Presbyterians some time after 1804.

NEWCASTLE-UNDER-LYME (Meth NC), Merrial Street, erec 1799, replaced by the Ebenezer Chapel in 1857. OR C 1812-37, 1859-1969 (NPL).

NEWCASTLE-UNDER-LYME (Meth NC), Marsh Chapel, Marsh Street, reg 1799.

NEWCASTLE-UNDER-LYME (Prim Meth), Chorlton Moss, erec 1833.

NEWCASTLE-UNDER-LYME (Prim Meth), Higherland, f 1823. OR ZC 1824-37 (PRO). COP ZC 1824-37 Mf (NPL), C 1824-37 (IGI).

NEWCASTLE-UNDER-LYME (Wes), Lower Street, erec 1799. Replaced by Brunswick Chapel about 1859. OR ZC 1804-13, 1804-37, B 1813-37 (note two sequences for early baptisms) (PRO), C 1886-1938 (NPL). COP ZC 1804-13, 1804-37, B 1813-37 Mf (NPL), C 1804-37 (IGI).

NEWCASTLE-UNDER-LYME, The Ireland. A nonconformist chapel was registered in 1828 but no denomination was given.

NEWCHAPEL St James (L). Chapelry to Wolstanton until 1846 and formerly called Thursfield Chapel. OR C 1723-1906, M 1742-54, 1847-1910, B 1724-1897, Banns 1897-1964 (SRO). BT 1726-1850 (gaps 1731, 1763-65, 1783-1804, 1810-12, 1846-54, no marriages recorded after 1755) (LJRO). COP C 1789-1812, B 1774-89 Ms (WSL), Extr C 1726-82, 1805-09, 1814-56 (IGI).

NEWHALL. See under STAPENHILL.

NEWSTONE (Wes). See under ALSTONFIELD.

NEWTON (Ind). See under HANDSWORTH.

NORBURY St Peter (L) (370). OR C 1538-1813, M 1538-1753, B 1538-1813 (Inc), CB 1813+ M 1754+ (Inc). BT 1673-1868 (gaps 1676-79, 1854, 1856) (LJRO). COP CMB 1538-1643 Ms (WSL), M 1538-1643 (SMI). Extr C 1673-1809, 1813-68, M 1673-1809, 1813-38, 1842-52 (IGI).

NORTHWOOD (Wes Meth Assoc). See under HANLEY.

NORTON CANES St James alias Norton under Cannock (L) (678). Peculiar of the Prebend of Handsacre and Armitage. OR CMB 1566+ (Inc). BT 1659-1859 (gaps 1662-68, 1675-79, 1681-84, 1687-88, 1741-44, 1838); the following years headed Norton and Wyrley 1714-24, 1727-32, 1735-41, 1747-50, 1753-56, 1759-65, 1768-71 (LJRO). COP Extr C 1659-1859, M 1659-1836 (IGI).

NORTON CANES (Ind), Brownhills erec 1816.

NORTON-IN-THE-MOORS St Bartholomew (L) (2407). Chapel to Stoke-on-Trent until 1807. OR C 1574-1905, M 1574-1912, B 1574-1905, Banns 1823-51, 1892-1904 (SRO). BT 1660-1852 (gaps 1667, 1669-77, 1747-51, 1767-70). COP CMB 1574-1751, 1754-1837 ptd (SPRS), CMB 1752-1812 Ms (WSL), M 1574-1812, M 1574-1751, 1754-1837 (CMI), Extr C 1575-1751, 1813-18 (IGI).

NORTON-IN-THE-MOORE (Ind), Milton, f 1808.

NORTON-IN-THE-MOORE (Meth NC), Milton, reg 1819.

NORTON-IN-THE-MOORS (Wes), Sandy Lane, erec 1805. OR Baptismal entries may be included in the Circuit Register for Burslem, Swan Bank (Wes).

NORTON-IN-THE-MOORS (Wes), Adamscroft, reg 1807. OR Baptismal entries may be included in the Circuit Register for Burslem, Swan Bank (Wes).

NORTON-IN-THE-MOORS (Wes), Brown Edge, erec before 1804. OR Baptismal
entries may be included in the Circuit Register for Burslem, Swan Bank (Wes).

NORTON UNDER CANNOCK St James. See under NORTON CANES St James/

OAKAMORE Holy Trinity (L). Chapelry to Cheadle becoming a parish in 1864, erec
1832. OR CMB 1832+ (Inc). BT 1835-55 (LJRO). COP Extr C 1835-55 (IGI).

OCKER HILL (Wes). See under TIPTON.

OFFLEY HIGH St Mary. See under HIGH OFFLEY.

OKEOVER All Saints (L) (62). OR C 1759-1930, M 1759-1940, B 1759-1955, Banns
1759-1801, 1850-1922 (SRO). BT 1737-1855 (LJRO). COP 1737-1955 Ps
(LJRO).

OLD HILL (Wes). See under ROWLEY REGIS.

OLD OSCOTT (RC). See under HANDSWORTH.

ONECOTE St Luke, erec 1751. Chapelry to Leek becoming a praish jointly with
Bradnop in 1862. (L). OR CMB 1755+ (Inc). BT 1782-1835 (LJRO).

ONECOTE (Prim Meth), erec 1822.

OSCOTT (RC). See under HANDSWORTH.

OVER ARLEY. See under ARLEY UPPER.

OVER TEAN (Ind), Providence Chapel. See under CHECKLEY.

PATSHULL St Mary (L) (132). OR C 1559-1812, M 1559-1835, B 1559-1812 (SRO),
CB 1812+ M 1835+ (Inc). BT 1656-1874 (gaps 1762-73, 1786-91, 1833-34, 1842-
43, M 1850-74, CB 1858-59, 1862 (LJRO). COP CMB 1560-1812 Ms (WSL),
Extr C 1656-64, 1682-1874 (IGI).

PATTINGHAM St Chad (L) (817). OR C 1559-1838, M 1559-1839, B 1559-1853
(SRO), BT 1660-1874 (gaps 1854-55, 1858-59) (LJRO). COP CMB 1559-1812 (I)
ptd (SPRS), M 1559-1812 (CMI, SMI), Extr C 1559-1874, M 1559-1812, 1814-50
(IGI).

PELSALL, formerly St Mary now St Michael & All Angels (L). Chapelry to
Wolverhampton. Royal Peculiar of Wolverhampton. OR C 1756-1946, M 1849-
1950, B 1756-1812, 1818-1946 (SRO). No earlier marriages. BT CB 1799-1839
(LJRO). COP Extr C 1799-1839 (IGI).

PELSALL (Wes), erec 1836.

PENKHULL (Prim Meth). See under STOKE-ON-TRENT.

PENKRIDGE St Michael (L) (2991). Royal Peculiar of Penkridge. OR C 1572-1967,
M 1572-1967, B 1572-1924 (SRO). BT 1673-1869 (gaps 1676-87, 1696-99, 1708-
11, 1716-20, M 1741-53, M 1855+), 1714-17 damaged (LJRO). COP CMB 1575-
1735 ptd (SPRS), CB 1572-1790, M 1572-1755 Ms (WSL), Extr C 1575-1740,
1804-69, M 1572-1740, 1813-55 (IGI), M 1575-1735 (SMI). See also under
SHARESHILL and STRETTON, COPPENHALL and DUNSTON.

PENKRIDGE (Prim Meth), Whiston Chapel, erec 1828.

PENKRIDGE (Wes), New Street, erec 1828.

PENN St Bartholomew (L) (863). OR C 1569-1876, M 1569-1845, B 1569-1852 (SRO).
BT 1664-1852 (gaps 1667-70, 1770-73, 1810-12) (LJRO). COP CMB 1570-1754
(I) ptd (SPRS), CMB 1748-1840 with Shenstone Ms (WSL), M 1570-1754 (SMI,
CMI), Extr C 1569-1809, 1813-52, M 1570-1753 (IGI).

PENSNETT. See under KINGSWINFORD.

PENSNETT CHASE (Pres). See under KINGSWINFORD.

48

PERRY BARR St John, erec 1833 (L). Chapelry to Handsworth. OR C 1833-1964, M 1864-1976, B 1834-1931 (BRL). BT 1834-68 (gap 1840) (LJRO).

PIPE RIDWARE St James. See under RIDWARE.

PORTABELLO (Wes). See under WILLENHALL.

QUARNFORD, Flash Chapel (L). Chapel to Alstonfield, erec 1744. OR C 1744-1847, B 1744-1870 (SRO). BT 1795-1864 (gaps 1859-63) (LJRO). COP Extr C 1821-54 (IGI).

QUARNFORD (Wes), Flash, reg 1799.

QUARRY BANK. See under KINGSWINFORD.

RAMSOR (Prim Meth). See under ELLASTONE.

RANTON All Saints (L) (290). Also spelt Ronton. OR C 1655-1885, M 1655-1916, B 1655-1812 (SRO), B 1812+ (Inc). BT 1660-1868 (gaps 1840-54) (LJRO). COP CMB 1655-1812 (I) ptd (SPRS), M 1655-1812 (CMI), M 1754-1812 (SMI), Extr C 1655-1868, M 1655-1812 (IGI).

RANTON (Wes), erec 1830.

RIDWARE HAMSTALL St Michael (L) (443). OR CMB 1598+ (Inc). BT 1662-1883 (gaps 1668-70), 1751-59, 1773-76, 1858-65) (LJRO). COP CMB 1598-1812 (I) ptd (SPRS), M 1741-1812 (SMI), M 1598-1812 (CMI), Extr C 1598-1856, M 1598-1832 (IGI).

RIDWARE MAVESYN St Nicholas (L) (576). Peculiar of the Dean of Lichfield. OR C 1538-1771, 1813-57, M 1538-1838, B 1538-1771 (SRO). BT 1663-1869 (gaps 1667, 1671, 1678-80, 1725-26, 1790-91, 1836, 1853) (LJRO). COP CMB 1538-1812 Ms (WSL), Extr M 1796-1843 (IGI).

RIDWARE MAVESYN, Hill Ridware. A nonconformist chapel was registered in 1825 but no denomination was given.

RIDWARE PIPE St James (L) (111). OR CMB 1571+ (Inc). BT 1659-1868 (gaps 1663-74, 1690-92, 1745-46, 1837-48, 1850-52, 1857) (LJRO). COP CMB 1571-1812 (I) ptd (SPRS), M 1571-1812 (CMI), Extr C 1571-1869, M 1565-1835 (IGI).

ROCESTER St Michael (L) (1040). OR CMB 1564-1812, Banns 1754-1802, 1823-62 (SRO), CMB 1812+ (Inc). BT 1674-1868 (gaps 1698-1701, 1810-12, 1848-50, 1853-55) (LJRO). COP CMB 1565-1812 ptd (SPRS), M 1565-1812 (SMI, CMI), Extr C 1565-1868, M 1565-1847 (IGI).

ROCESTER (Gen Bapt), erec 1837.

ROCESTER (Prim Meth), erec 1812.

ROLLESTON St Mary (L) (866). Also spelt Roulston. OR CMB 1569+ (Inc). BT 1662-1868 (gaps 1670-71, 1673, 1747-51, 1846-47, 1851, 1856-63) (LJRO), note 1791-95 in terriers. COP Extr C 1662-1809, 1813-66, M 1662-1809, 1813-35 (IGI).

ROLLESTON (Prim Meth), Anslow, erec 1829.

ROLLESTON (Wes), erec 1801, another erec before 1820.

ROLLESTON (Wes), Anslow Lees, erec 1808.

ROLLESTON (Wes), Anslow, erec 1810.

RONTON. See under RANTON.

ROULSTON. See under ROLLESTON.

ROWLEY REGIS St Giles (W) (7438), chapelry to Clent until 1842. OR CMB 1539-1684, 1714-1970 (up to 1912 damaged by fire, very fragile and cannot normally be handled) (SPL). BT 1606-1874 (WRO). COP CMB 1539-1812 (I) ptd (SPRS), C

1813-59 (I) Ms (SPL), p/c of damaged registers C 1539-1684, 1714-1912, M 1539-1684, 1714-1812 (SPL), M 1685-1714 (Boyd Misc), M 1539-1812 (SMI, CMI), M 1813-1900 (SPL), Extr C 1539-1812, M 1539-1812 (IGI).

ROWLEY REGIS (Bapt), Providence Chapel, erec 1823.

ROWLEY REGIS (Gen Bapt), Cradley Heath, Five Ways, f 1832.

ROWLEY REGIS (Meth NC), Providence Tabernacle, Tividale, erec 1837.

ROWLEY REGIS (Meth NC), Bethel Chapel, Cradley Heath, Five Ways, f 1826. The Bethel Chapel was built in Scholding in 1836 and replaced by Christ Church, Five Ways in 1885. OR M 1905-60 (SRO).

ROWLEY REGIS (Prim Meth), Brethill, erec 1828. OR Register for Brierley Hill, Round Oak includes some Rowley Regis entries.

ROWLEY REGIS (Prim Meth), f 1821. Cradley Heath now Graingers Lane. OR 1848+ (Inc). Early entries may be included in the Circuit Register. See under BRIERLEY HILL, Round Oak.

ROWLEY REGIS (Wes), Old Hill, erec 1830.

RUGELEY St Augustine (L) (3165). Peculiar of the Dean and Chapter of Lichfield. OR C 1569-1905, M 1569-1895, B 1569-1882, Banns 1823-90 (SRO). BT 1659-1880 (gaps 1681-84, 1735-38, M 1780-95). COP CMB 1569-1722 (I) ptd (SPRS), CMB 1721-1812 Ms (WSL), M 1569-1722 (CMI), Extr C 1569-1721, (BT) 1819-75, M 1569-1721, 1819-37 (IGI). See also under BRERETON.

RUGELEY St Joseph & Ethelreda (RC). OR C 1836+ (DA).

RUGELEY (S of F), Albion Street, erec 1830.

RUGELEY (Ind), Providence Chapel, Elmore Lane, erec 1813. OR ZC 1821-37 (PRO). COP C 1821-37 Mf (SRO), C 1821-37 (IGI).

RUGELEY (Meth), Reg 1808.

RUITON (Ind). See under GORNAL UPPER.

RUSHALL St Michael (L) (693). OR C 1686+ M 1734-69, 1772+ B 1771+ (Inc). BT 1660-1868 (gaps 1660-92 (small gaps), 1693-98, 1713-15, 1741-44, 1770-76) (LJRO). COP C 1686-1812, M 1734-69, B "no entry for burials found prior to 1771" (Willmore "Records of Rushall", SG), Extr C 1660-1868, M 1660-1837 (IGI).

RUSHTON SPENCER St Lawrence (L). Chapel to Leek becoming a parish in 1864. OR C 1700-1908, M 1700-1837, B 1700-1851 (SRO). BT 1693-1875 (gaps 1700-07) (LJRO). COP Extr C 1693-1856, M 1693-1811, 1820-36 (IGI).

RUSHTON SPENCER (Prim Meth) (Bapt). Primitive Methodists had Cloud Chapel near to Woodhouse Green on the plan in 1811. The Baptists had the right to use the same building and were doing so in 1828. There was an associated burial ground with memorial stones dating to 1672. The last burial was in 1780.

SALT. See under STAFFORD.

SANDON All Saints (L) (558). OR C 1635-1843, M 1635-1856, B 1635-1873, Banns 1754-1822 (SRO). BT 1660-1868 (gaps 1705-09, 1710-11, 1810-12, 1836, 1860, 1865, 1867) (LJRO). COP C 1660-1805, 1813-68, M 1661-1805, 1813-50 (IGI).

SANDON. A nonconformist chapel was registered in 1822 but no denomination was given.

SEDGLEY All Saints (L) (20,577). Peculiar of the Manor of Sedgley. OR C 1558-1899, M 1558-1904, B 1558-1900, Banns 1870-72 (SRO). BT 1673-1853 (gaps 1711-14, 1733, M 1793-94, C 1803, M 1837-53) note there are some discrepancies in marriage entries between OR's & BT's (LJRO). COP CMB

1558-1684 ptd (SPRS), CMB 1701-1812 (mf of OR) (SRO), CB 1685-1781 (I) Ms
(WSL), CB 1558-1701, 1754-81, M 1700-54 Ms (SG), CMB 1701-34 Ms (DPL),
CMB 1685-1701, M 1701-81 Ms (WoPL), Extr CMB 1558-1600 (BRL), Index M
1701-54, B 1823 (BMSGH), Index C 1701-1819, M 1558-1633, 1685-1837, B
1701-1823 (SRO), M 1558-1684 (CMI), M 1702-54 (SMI), Extr C 1558-1786, 1809-
53, M 1558-1685, 1786-1837 (IGI). See also under COSELEY, ETTINGSHALL
and GORNAL.

SEDGLEY St Chad & All Saints (RC). OR C 1795+ M 1817+ D 1801+ B 1823+
Confms 1807+ (DA).

SEDGLEY (RC), private chapel attached to Sedgley Park erected about 1763. OR
Confirmation lists only in the Bishop's registers.

SEDGLEY (Part Bapt), Coppice also called Coppia, f 1804. OR Births &
namings1798, Z1820-37 (PRO). COP Namings 1794-1820, C & namings 1818-37
Ms (DPL), Z 1796-1834 Mf (SRO), Extr Z 1794-1837 (IGI).

SEDGLEY (Meth NC), Mount Zion Chapel, erec before 1800, another erec 1835.

SEDGLEY (Wes), Hurst Hill, Cann Lane, erec 1798. OR Early entries may be
included in Bilston register (q.v.), C 1848+ M 1901+ (Inc Hurst Hill Methodist
Church, Bilston).

SEDGLEY (Wes), Lean Lane, erec 1798.

SEIGHFORD St Chad (L) (898). OR C 1560-1879, M 1560-1837, B 1560-1925 (note
that the first register contains entries CMB 1560-1656 with no entries 1636-
53. The second register covers CMB 1642-1744 with a note at the front that
the register was bought by the churchwardens in 1656 and the entries 1642-53
were "restored" from papers left by the Parish Clerk), Banns 1754-1812 (SRO).
BT 1661-1850 (LJRO). COP CMB 1561-1812 (gaps 1636-42, 1664-73), Banns
1756-1812 for those not married in the parish, ptd (SPRS), M 1561-1812 (SMI),
Extr C 1661-1809, 1813-50, M 1661-1809, 1813-42 (IGI).

SEISDON. See under TRYSULL.

SHALLOWFORD (S of F). See under CHEBSEY.

SHARESHILL St Mary, formerly ST Luke (L) (520). Chapel to Pankrdige. Royal
Peculiar of Wolverhampton. OR C 1565-1849, M 1565-1959, B 1565-1951 (gaps
CMB 1644-47), Banns 1754-1820, 1823-1964 (SRO). BT 1687-1868 (gaps 1695-
99, 1701-03, 1709-18, 1721-25, 1731-35, M 1797-1812, 1832, 1837-58) (LJRO).
COP CMB 1564-1812, M 1813-38 Ms (WSL), CMB 1565-1754, CB 1754-1812 Mf
(SRO), Extr C 1813-68, M 1813-36 (IGI).

SHEEN St Luke (L) (368). OR C 1595-1865, M 1595-1836, B 1595-1812, Banns 1756-
1801 (SRO), B1813+ (Inc). BT 1660-1852 (parts of 1795-1800 missing) (LJRO).
COP Extr CM 1660-1852 (IGI).

SHELTON St Mark (L). Chapelry to Stock-on-Trent, erec 1834. OR CB 1834+ M
1839+ (Inc). BT 1834-36 (LJRO). See also under HANLEY.

SHELTON (Ind), Hope Street, erec 1810. OR ZC 1809-37 (PRO). COP ZC 1809-37
Mf (HPL), Extr C 1809-37 (IGI).

SHELTON (Ind), Brunswick Chapel, Sackville Street, erec 1824. Formed as a
secession of Hope Street Independent Chapel, it became Presbyterian in 1846.

SHELTON (Unit), Hill Street, reg 1823, closed 1831.

SHELTON (Meth NC), Bethesda Chapel, Albion Street, erec 1798. OR ZC 1797-1837
(PRO), C 1797-1920, M 1838-99, B 1837-1930, register of interments 1824-55,
register of members 1828-74 (HPL-prior notice needed). COP ZC 1797-1821
Mf (HPL), C 1810-37 Mf (Hanley Circuit) (HPL), Extr C 1797-1837 (IGI).

SHELTON (Meth NC), Bedford Chapel, erec 1834.

SHELTON (Meth NC), Etruria, reg 1819.

SHELTON (Wes), Etruria, erec 1808.

SHENSTONE St John the Baptist (L) (1827). OR C 1579-1860, M 1579-1837, B 1579-1890 (gap CMB 1611-54), Banns 1785-1806 (SRO). BT 1653-1910 (gaps 1674, C 1679, M 1679-81, 1759-61) (LJRO). COP CMB 1579-1812 Ms (WSL), Extr C 1653-1875, M 1813-37 (IGI). See also STONNALL.

SHENSTONE (S of F), Lynn, f 1672. Member of Stafford MM.

SHERIFF HALES St Mary (L) (914). Formerley in Staffs now in Salop. OR CMB 1557+ (Inc). BT 1670-1859 (gaps 1672-77, 1679-93, 1726-30, 1741-44) (LJRO). COP CMB 1557-1812 ptd (Shropshire PRS), M 1551-1812 (Boyds Shropshire), Extr CM 1557-1812 (IGI-listed under Shropshire).

SHOOTERS HILL. See under WOLVERHAMPTON.

SHUTT END (Prim Meth). See under KINGSWINFORD, Pensnett.

SMETHWICK Old Church (L), Chapel to Harborne, erec 1723. OR CMB 1732+ (Inc). BT 1774-1857 (gaps 1795-98, 1801-04, 1846, B 1847, 1854; CB only recorded although one marriage in 1786, one in 1789 and 14 in 1848 (LJRO). COP p/s CB 1774-95, 1798-1801, 1804-45, 1848-53, 1856-57 (SPL), Extr C 1774-1857 (IGI).

SMETHWICK (Ind), Berewood's Hill, erec 1823.

SMETHWICK (Prim Meth). Register for Brierley Hill, Round Oak includes some Smethwick entries.

SMETHWICK (Wes), erec 1824.

SNEYD GREEN (Wes). See under BURSLEM.

STAFFORD St Chad (L) (6956 including St Mary). OR C 1636-1888, M 1636-1923, B 1636-1859 (SRO). BT 1636-1864 (gaps 1639-71, 1679-81, 1687-90, 1693-95, 1721-27, 1772-85, 1793-95, 1805-13, 1855) (LJRO). COP CMB 1636-1811 (I) ptd (SPRS), M 1636-1811 (SMI, CMI), Extr C 1636-1864, M 1636-42, 1662-1736, 1748-1811, 1813-14, 1824-48 (IGI).

STAFFORD St Mary (L). OR CM 1559-1903, B 1559-1878, Banns 1823-40, 1853-57 (SRO). BT 1673-1868 (gaps 1677-78, 1683, 1698-1701, 1810-12, M 1851-68, CB 1854, 1857, 1865) (LJRO). COP CMB 1559-1671 (I) ptd (SPRS), CMB 1559-1812 Mf (SRO), CMB 1700-1823 Ms (SG), M 1559-1671 (SMI, CMI), Extr C 1559-1671, 1673-1809, 1813-68, M 1559-1671, 1673-1809, 1813-51 (IGI).

STAFFORD Castle Church (L) (1374). OR C 1567-1887, M 1567-1883, B 1573-1882, Banns 1757-1812, 1851-1952 (SRO). BT 1680-1868 (gaps 1705-08, 1722-26, 1751-62, 1853, 1857-60) (LJRO). COP CMB 1568-1812 ptd (SPRS), M 1568-1812 (CMI), Extr CM 1568-1856, C 1862-68 (IGI). See also under ACTION TRUSSELL, BEDNALL and MARSTON.

STAFFORD St Austins (RC), Forebridge, erec 1791. OR C 1804+ M 1832+ D 1831+ (Inc).

STAFFORD (S of F), Foregate Street, Monthly Meeting. OR Minute Book containing list of members 1814 and 1818, record of sufferings 1688-1785, 1793-1838, drafts and individual sufferings 1744-92, 1830-35, 1846, 1860-61, list of members 1829 and C 1837, disownments, condemnations, particularly marriages out 1679-1766, correspondence book on movements 1701-1838, removal certs and acknowledgements 1784-1839, birth notes submitted to Stafford MM 1837-65, burial notes at Stafford MM 1836-61, miscellaneous membership papers 1801-1968, list of subscribers for purchase of meeting house late 17th.c, account books 1795-1375, Extr Cheshire & Staffs QM 1828-39, Stafford PM minutes 1787-1913, minute books 1713-83, 1801-49 (SRO).

STAFFORD (Part Bapt), parish of St Mary, erec before 1800.

STAFFORD (Ind), Zion Chapel, St Martin Street, but before 1811 in Salters Street, f
1786. OR ZC 1795-1828, C 1829-1837 (PRO). COP ZC 1795-1828, C 1829-
1837 (Mf (SRO), Extr C 1788-1837 (IGI).

STAFFORD (Pres), Mount Street, Bulk Passage, f 1687. Closed about 1810 although
opened again in 1851, shared minister with Stone.

STAFFORD (Meth NC), County Road, erec 1816. Chapel replaced by Snow Hill
Chapel in Foregate in 1849.

STAFFORD (Prim Meth), f 1837.

STAFFORD (Wes), Broad Chapel, erec 1811, in parish of St. Mary. OR ZC 1809-37
(PRO). COP C 1809-37 (IGI).

STAFFORD, Salt. A nonconformist chapel was registered in 1816 but no
denomination was given.

STAFFORDSHIRE (RC). OR Confirmation lists - Bishop's Confirmation Register
1768-1816 (DA). COP Bishops Confirmation Register 1768-1816 ptd (Staffs
Cath Hist No 12.1972). Some Staffs entries included in Westminster
Cathedral, C 1729-1827, M 1729-54 Mf (SG).

STAFFORDSHIRE & CHIESHIRE Quarterly Meeting (S of F). See under CHESHIRE
& STAFFORDSHIRE (S of F).

STAFFORDSHIRE Quarterly Meeting (S of F). IN 1783 the QM was amalgamated as
the Cheshire & Staffordshire QM. OR Minute books 1672-1783, 1784-1820 (the
latter entries probably refer to the Stafford and Leek MM), draft minute book
1734/5-76, minutes of women's QM 1764-82 (at rear of Uttoxeter women's
meeting book) (SRO).

STANDON All Saints (L) (420). OR C 1558-77, M 1558-1863, B 1558-96 (SRO). BT
1679-1856 (gap CB 1856), note 1786-91 in terriers (LJRO). COP CMB 1558-
1812 (I) ptd (SPRS), Extr CMB 1558-1758 ptd 1888 (History of Standon, Ed.
Salt), M 1558-1812 (CMI, SMI), Extr CM 1558-1812 (IGI).

STANLEY. See under ENDON.

STANTON. See under ELLASTONE.

STAPENHILL St Peter (L). Transferred in 1894 to Staffs from Derbyshire. OR C
1679-1912, M 1679-1923, B 1679-1872 (Derby RO). BT 1663-1869 (gaps 1748-
61, 1770-1800, 1811-12) (LJRO). COP C 1813-56, M 1813-37 (IGI - listed under
Derbyshire).

STEPENHILL, Newhall. Chapelry to St Peter. BT 1833-82 (LJRO).

STAPENHILL (Wes), erec 1834.

STAPENHILL (Wes), Newhall, erec 1816.

STATFOLD All Saints. A small church standing in the grounds of the Hall, the
residence of the Stanley-Pipe-Wolferstan family. Until 1906 when it was
refitted for use as a parish church, it had long been used merely as a mortuary
chapel for that family.

STOKE-ON-TRENT. This was the largest parish in the County until an Act passed in
1807 entitled "An Act for separating the Chapelries and Chapels of Newcastle-
under-Lyme, Burslem, Whitmore, Bucknall-cum-Bagnall and Norton-in-the-
Moors from the Rectory and Parish Church of Stoke-upon-Trent and for making
them five distinct Rectories ..." In 1827, an Act allowed an ecclesiastical sub-
division to form Shelton and Longton.

STOKE-ON-TRENT St Peter & Vincula (L) (37,200). OR C 1629-1770, 1798-1857, M
1629-1837, B 1629-1773, 1798-1840 (containing Hanley CB 1744-47) (SRO). BT

1679-1837 (gaps M 1679, 1755-58, 1766-70, 1832, M 1833-37) containing entries for Bucknall (C 1758-62), Bagnall (C 1758-62), Bagnall (C 1758-62), Hanley (CB 1744-47), some Stoke marriages included in Whitmore's BT's 1754-1801. (LJRO). COP CMB 1629-1812 ptd (SPRS-containing Hanley CB 1743-46, 1748), C 1812-57, M 1812-37, B 1812-40 Ms (HPL), M 1629-1797 (SMI), M 1629-1812 (CMI), Extr C 1629-1838, M 1629-1837 (IGI).

STOKE-ON-TRENT (S of F), Thomas Street. Chapel originally built in 1823 as Independent later becoming S of F. OR PM minutes 1852-79 (SRO).

STOKE-ON-TRENT (Ind). See above.

STOKE-ON-TRENT (Meth NC), Mount Zion Chapel, erec 1815 replacing the Cross Street Chapel which was erected in 1799. OR C 1842+ (Inc). Entries for Stoke-on-Trent are included in Longton Circuit Register for which see under LONGTON.

STOKE-ON-TRENT (Meth NC), Epworth Street, OR C 1813-1938 (SRO). Entries for Stoke-on-Trent also appear in Longton Circuit Register for which see under LONGTON.

STOKE-ON-TRENT (Meth NC), Eastwood Vale Chapel, erec 1827. Entries for Stoke-on-Trent appear in the Longton Circuit Register for which see under LONGTON.

STOKE-ON-TRENT (Meth NC), Mount Tabor Chapel, Market Street, Fenton, erec 1811. Entries for Stoke-on-Trent appear in Longton Circuit Registers for which see under LONGTON.

STOKE-ON-TRENT (Meth NC), Harpsfield, erec 1833. Entries for Stoke-on-Trent appear in the Longton Circuit Register for which see under LONGTON.

STOKE-ON-TRENT (Math NC), Lightwood. See under STONE.

STOKE-ON-TRENT (Prim Meth), Cobermare, Leese Street (formerly known as John St) erec 1834.

STOKE-ON-TRENT (Prim Meth), Penkhull, f 1832. OR ZC 1832-37 (PRO). COP 1832-37 Mf (SRO), Extr C 1832-37 (IGI).

STOKE-ON-TRENT (Wes), Fenton, erec 1812. A later chapel was erected in Temple Street in 1831. OR ZC 1799-1837 (PRO). COP ZC 1799-1837 Mf (HPL), Extr C 1799-1837 (IGI).

STOKE-ON-TRENT (Wes), Sedgley Chapel, f 1799. OR ZC 1813-37 (PRO). COP Extr C 1813-37 (IGI).

STOKE-ON-TRENT, Hartshill Common. A nonconformist chapel was registered in 1807 but no denomination was given.

STONE St Michael (L) (7808). OR CMB 1568+ (Inc). BT 1668-1892 (gaps 1671-72, 1677-78, 1693, 1809-12); these include some Fulford BT's and also some entries for Hilderstone (LJRO). COP CMB 1569-1812 including Fulford Mf (SRO), Extr C 1813-75, M 1813-52 (IGI). See also under FULFORD and HILDERSTONE.

STONE (RC), Aston. Aston Hall was used by RC's but later was replaced by St Michael's church. OR C 1804+ M 1833+ Confms 1820+ (Inc). COP C 1804+ M 1833+ Confms 1820+ Ms (DA).

STONE (Ind), Chapel Street, f 1787 OR ZC 1787-1837 (PRO). COP ZC 1787-1837 Mf (SRO), Extr C 1787-1837 (IGI).

STONE (Pres), f 1705. Shared minister with Stafford from 1748 and closed 1808.

STONE (Meth NC), Mount Zion, erec 1816. Another chapel was erected at Stone 1836. OR Some Stone entries appear in the Longton Circuit register for which see under LONGTON.

STONE (Meth NC), Zoar Chapel, Abbey Court, erec 1821. OR Some Stone entries
appear in the Circuit register under LONGTON which see.

STONE (Meth NC), Lightwood, reg 1819. Lightwood is now in Stoke-on-Trent. OR
Some Stone entries appear in the Longton Circuit Register for which see under
LONGTON.

STONE (Wes), Lichfield Street, f 1827.

STONNALL St Peter, erec 1822. Chapelry to Shenstone becoming a parish in 1845.
OR C 1823+ M 1846+ B 1823+ (Inc). BT 1823-36 (LJRO). COP C (BT) 1823-36
(IGI).

STONYLOW (S of F). See under MADELEY.

STOWE-BY-CHARTLEY St John the Baptist (L) (1283). OR C 1575-1943, M 1575-
1837, B 1575-1866 (SRO). BT 1679-1867 (gaps 1762-66, 1849) (LJRO). COP
CMB 1613-89 ptd (SPRS), CMB 1574-1672 Ms (SG), M 1613-89 (SMI, CMI), Extr
C 1574-1867, M 1613-1858 (IGI).

STOWE-BY-LICHFIELD. See under LICHFIELD St Chad.

STRETTON St John (L). Chapelry to Penkridge. Royal Peculiar of Penkridge. OR
C 1659-1958, M 1659-1837, B 1659-1973, Banns 1824-1870 (SRO). BT 1678-
1893 (gaps 1681-90, 1696-1706, 1708-14, 1716-24, 1727-28, 1731-32, 1734-38, M
1740-88, 1792-1804, 1809-10) (LJRO). COP CMB 1659-1812 Ms (WSL), Extr C
1678-1877, M 1692-96, 1714-16, 1728-34, 1804-37 (IGI).

SWAN BANK (Wes). See under BILSTON.

SWINDON (Ind). See under WOMBOURNE.

SWINNTERTON. See under SWYNNERTON.

SWINSCOE (Prim Meth). See under BLORE.

SWYNNERTON St Mary (L) 791). OR CMB 1558+ (Inc). BT 1675-1868 (gaps 1679-
85, 1810-12) (LJRO). COP CMB 1558-1812 Mf (SRO), CMB 1558-1812 Ms
(WSL), C 1810-42, M 1816-41, B 1813-19 Ms (BMSGH), M 1558-1812 (SMI), Extr
C 1676-1809, 1813-68, M 1676-1809, 1813-48 (IGI).

SWYNNERTON (RC) St Mary, reg 1791. OR C 1810+ M 1816+ D 1813-19 (Inc). COP
C 1810-42, M 1826-41, B 1813-19 Ms (SG).

TALKE-O'-TH'-HILL St Martin, formerly a chapelry to Audley (L). OR CMB 1830+
(Inc). BT 1786-91. The following are included under Audley: CB 1722-30,
1730-35, 1744-46, 1782-86, 1791-1812 and post 1812 (LJRO). COP C 1786-91
(IGI).

TALKE-O'-TH'-HILL (Prim Meth), erec 1813.

TALKE-O'-TH'-HILL (Wes), Red Street, erec 1833. This chapel was registered as
Red Street, Wedgewood Place, Knowle End, Audley.

TAMWORTH St Editha (L) (3917). This parish was half in Warwickshire and half in
Staffordshire until 1890 when it became wholly part of Staffordshire. OR CMB
1556+ (Inc). BT 1664-1868 (gaps 1712-14, M 1766-73, M 1795-1800, 1810-12, M
1845-68, CB 1865) (LJRO). COP CMB 1558-1614 ptd (SPRS), CMB 1556-1860
Mf (SRO), CMB 1614-35 Ms (WSL), M 1558-1614 (SMI, CMI), Extr C 1556-1614,
1714-1809, 1813-68, M 1557-1614, 1813-44 (IGI). See also under FAZELEY and
WIGGINTON.

TAMWORTH St John the Baptist (RC), St John's Place, Aldergate Street, reg 1830.
OR C 1826+ (Inc).

TAMWORTH (S of F), Lichfield Street. From 1668 to 1710 this was in the Wishaw
(afterwards Baddesley) MM. From 1719 to 1852 it was in the Birmingham
(afterwards Warwickshire North) MM. OR Registers for the Wishaw MM are at

the PRO (Warwickshire), those for the Birmingham MM are at Friends House, Bull Street, Birmingham.

TAMWORTH (Part Bapt), Lichfield Street, reg 1794. The chapel was originally in Bewbridge (later Bolebridge) Street moving to Peel Street in 1799.

TAMWORTH (Ind), Aldergate Street, erec 1827. OR ZC 1827-36 (PRO under Warwickshire). COP ZC 1827-36 Mf (SRO), C 1827-36 (IGI).

TAMWORTH (Unit), Colehill, f 1724 (formerly Presbyterian). OR C 1695-1837, B 1822-36 (PRO listed under Warwickshire).

TAMWORTH (Wes), Bewbridge (later Bolebridge) Street also called Bole Street, reg 1794. OR ZC 1800-25, 1800-37 (PRO). COP ZC 1800-36 Mf (SRO), Extr C 1800-37 (IGI).

TATENHILL St Michael & All Angels (L) (2180). OR C 1563-1849, M 1563-1837, B 1563-1878 (SRO). BT 1660-1868 (gaps 1712-13, 1806-08, 1857-63). COP CMB 1563-1812 ptd (SPRS), Index to CMB 1563-1812 Ms (WSL), M 1563-1812 (CMI), Extr C 1563-1868, M 1563-1868, M 1563-1841 (IGI).

SEE also under BARTON-UNDER-NEEDWOOD and WICHNOR.

TATENHILL (Wes), erec 1830.

TEAN. See under CHECKLEY.

TETTENHALL St Michael & All Angels (L) (2618). Also called Tettenhall Regis. Royal Peculiar of Tettenhall. OR CMB 1602-1915 (gaps M 1661-63, M 1728, M 1736, B 1662), Banns 1754-99 (SRO). BT 1687-1859 (gaps 1692-96, 1699-1715, 1717-1800, 1837) (LJRO). COP C 1602-1741, M 1602-1744, B 1602-1732 ptd (SPRS), M 1745-1839 ptd (SPRS), Index M 1745-1839 (WSL, SG), Index M 1601-1839 (BMSGH), C 1602-1797, M 1602-1839, B 1602-97 Ms (SG), M 1602-1839 (CMI), M 1745-1839 (SMI), Extr C 1602-1741, 1800-13, M 1602-1839 (IGI).

TETTENHALL (Ind), reg 1837.

TETTENHALL (Wes), Tettenhall Wood, erec 1825.

THORPE CONSTANTINE St Constatnine (L) (49). OR CMB 1539-1754, CB 1755-1812, Misc. papers MB 1785-1926, Communicants 1829-52 (SRO), CB 1812+ M 1755+ (Inc). BT 1662-1879 (gaps 1796-1804, 1864-73) (LJRO). COP Extr C 1667-1811, 1813-66 (IGI).

THURSFIELD St James. See under NEWCHAPEL.

TIPTON St Martin (L) (14,951). Peculiar of the Prebend of Prees. Originally, the church stood at Summer Hill near Princes End but as both church and burial ground were small, a new church was commenced in 1795 on a new site. St John's church was built on the original site in 1850. OR CMB 1573+ (Inc). BT 1672-1837 (gaps 1674-75, 1678-81, 1707-11, 1732-35) (LJRO). COP CMB 1513-1736 ptd (SPRS), (opening date given as 1513- see introduction to this listing), CMB 1736-1812 Ms (WSL), CMB 1575-1812 Ms (Tipton PL), CMB 1513-1812 Mf of OR (Tipton PL), M 1573-1736 (SMI, CMI), Extr C 1573-1837, M 1574-1736, 1813-37 (IGI).

TIPTON St Paul, Owen Street. No burial ground. OR CMB 1834+ (Inc).

TIPTON (Bapt), Mount Zion, Toll End, erec 1817.

TIPTON (Ind), Union Street. Used a house in Union Street in 1830. In 1832 part of the congregation formed the Ebenezer Chapel but re-united in 1837. A chapel was erected in 1833.

TIPTON (Meth NC), Canal Street, erec 1836.

TIPTON (Meth NC), St Paul's Chapel, Dudley Port, erec 1836.

TIPTON (Prim Meth), Upper Green Chapel, erec 1823.

TIPTON (Wes), Tipton Green, erec 1750. OR ZC 1809-37 (PRO Listed as Worcs). COP Extr C 1809-37 (IGI-listed as Staffs).

TIPTON (Wes), Bloomfield, erec 1820. OR ZC 1823-37 (PRO-listed as Worcs). COP Extr C 1823-37 (IGI-listed as Staffs).

TIPTON (Wes), Dudley Port, erec 1827.

TIPTON (Wes), Gospel Oak, erec 1811.

TIPTON (Wes), Great Bridge, erec 1811.

TIPTON (Wes), Ocker Hill, erec 1811.

TIVIDALE (Meth NC), Providence Tabernacle. See under ROWLEY REGIS.

TIXALL St John the Baptist (L) (176). OR CB 1707-1812, M 1707-1836, Banns 1823-1966 (SRO), CB 1813+ M 1837+ (Inc). BT 1663-1865 (gaps 1665-68, 1679, 1836, 1853-55) (LJRO). COP Extr C 1663-1809, 1813-65, M 1663-1809, 1813-51 (IGI).

TIXALL St John the Baptist (RC), f 1791. Bellamore was the private chapel of the Blount family and was attended by the Catholics of the area (Rugeley etc.) until the estate was sold. Then they went to Tixall, the property of the Clifford family who built a chapel, separate from the Hall in 1823. In 1845 this church was moved stone by stone and re-erected a Great Haywood. OR Bellamore C 1791-1821 (DA), Tixall C 1798-1837, M 1799-1853, B 1799-1830 (DA).

TOLL END (Bapt), Mount Zion. See under TIPTON.

TRENTHAM St Mary & All Saints (L) (2344). OR CMB 1558+ (gap 1640-56) (Inc). BT 1670-1852 (gaps 1673-80, C 1680-85, M 1683-91, 1752-57, 1763-65), 1800-05 are included in terriers (LJRO). BT's include Blurton C 1732-33, 1738-51, 1771-76, 1786-90, 1813-21). COP CB 1558-1812, M 1561-1812 ptd (SPRS), M 1561-1812 (SMI, CMI), Extr CM 1558-1852 (IGI). See also under BLURTON, HANFORD and WHITMORE.

TRYSULL All Saints including Seisdon (L) (562). OR C 1558-1855, M 1558-1933, B 1558-1880, pages to 1572 largely torn out (SRO). BT 1665-1868 (gaps 1663-69, 1673, 1693-97, M 1761-81, B 1771-72, M 1792, M 1829-30, 1837-38, 1841, 1853-55). COP CMB 1559-1812 Ms (WSL), Extr C 1730-1856, M 1730-1812, 1847-52 (IGI).

TUNSTALL Christ Church, High Street, erec 1832. Chapelry to Wolstanton (L). OR C 1822-1944, M 1838-1948, B 1832-1929 (SRO). BT 1832-68 (gaps 1840-52, 1854) (LJRO). COP Extr C 1832-68 (IGI).

TUNSTALL (Meth NC), Mount Taber Chapel, Market Square, erec 1824.

TUNSTALL (Prim Meth), erec 1811. OR ZC 1819-37 (PRO). COP ZC 1822-37 Mf (HPL), Extr C 1819-37 (IGI).

TUNSTALL (Wes), f 1795. OR ZC 1787-1837 (PRO). Note that some Tunstall entries appear in the Circuit register for Burslem, Swan Bank. COP C 1787-1837 Mf (NPL), Extr C 1787-1837 (IGI).

TUNSTALL (Sandemanians), reg 1812. Met for a few years.

TUTBURY St Mary (L) (1553). OR C 1668-1916, M 1754-1876, B 1668-1906 (SRO). BT 1673-1838 (gaps 1711-14, 1809-12, 1836) (LJRO). COP CMB 1673-1809 Ms (SG), CMB (BT) 1673-1809 Mf (HPL), Extr C 1673-1809, 1813-38, M 1673-1808, 1813-35 (IGI).

TUTBURY (S of F), reg 1700.

TUTBURY (Ind), Back Street, properly Monk Street, f 1799. OR ZC 1801-37 (PRO).

COP ZC 1801-37 Mf (SRO), Extr C 1801-37 (IGI).

TUTBURY (Prim Meth), reg 1818.

TUTBURY (Wes). OR C 1830-1919 (Manse, Farfield Road, Uttoxeter).

UPPER ARLEY. See under ARLEY UPPER.

UPPER ELKSTONE. See under ELKSTONE.

UPPER GORNAL. See under GORNAL.

UPPER HANLEY (Meth NC), Providence Chapel. See under HANLEY UPPER.

UPPER TEAN. See under CHECKLEY.

UTTOXETER St Mary (L) (4864). OR CMB 1596+ (Inc). BT 1668-1858 (gaps 1671-73, 1676-79, B 1682-85, CM 1684-85, M 1758-62, 1809-12) (LJRO). COP CMB 1596-1812 Mf (WSL), Extr M 1750-1835 Ms (SG), Extr CMB 1619-52 Ms (Inc), Extr C 1762-1809, 1813-56, M 1726-1809, 1813-56 (IGI).

UTTOXETER (RC), Balance Street, erec 1839. OR 1835+ (Inc).

UTTOXETER (S of F), Carter Street, reg 1705, MM. OR Periods covered in a variety of books: Z 1662-1836, M 1663-1835, B 1649-1837 (PRO), Minute Books Mens PM 1782-1869, Minute Books Womens PM 1783-95 at the back of which are Womens QM 1764-82, Minute Book Womens 1795-1839 (SRO).

UTTOXETER (Ind), Carter Street, formerly of Bear Hill, f 1792. OR ZC 1793-1836 (PRO). COP Extr C 1793-1836 (IGI).

UTTOXETER (Pres), reg 1718, f 1695.

UTTOXETER (Wes), High Street, erec 1812. OR ZC 1812-37 (PRO). COP ZC 1812-37 Mf (SRO), Extr C 1798-1837 (IGI).

WALSALL St Matthew (L) (15,066). OR CMB 1570+ (Inc). BT 1673-1858 (gaps M 1765-66, 1831-35, M 1848-58) (LJRO). COP C 1570-1645, M 1570-1649, B 1570-1648 ptd 1890 (FW Willmore, copies SRO, LJRO, BRL etc.), C 1646-1791, M 1676-1747, B 1662-78 Ms (WaPL), C 1646-75, M 1662-1754 Ms (SRO, SG), C 1648-1812 Ms (LJRO), Extr C 1570-1645, 1813-30, 1836-58, M 1570-1649, 1791-1830, 1836-47 (IGI), M 1662-1754 (SMI).

WALSALL St Paul's Propretary Chapel, erec 1826. Erected by the Governors of the New Grammar School, Queen Mary's Walsall. OR C 1874-1951, M 1875-1952 (SRO). BT 1843-55 (LJRO). See also under BLOXWICH and WALSALL WOOD.

WALSALL St Mary (RC), reg 1820. OR CM 1830+ (Inc). COP C 1762-66 taken from notebook of Pierce Parry, priest, a total of 17 entries, ptd (SPRS).

WALSALL (Bapt), Sutton Road, f 1831. Another at Goodall Street, erec 1833.

WALSALL (Part Bapt), Brod, erec 1836.

WALSALL (Ind), Bridge Street, f 1765. The chapel in Bridge Street was erected in 1790 in lieu of an older one in Dudley Street. OR ZC 1786-1837 (PRO). COP ZC 1786-1837 (Mf (SRO, WaPL), Extr C 1786-1837 (IGI).

WALSALL (Unit), f 1672. Chapel built in Stafford Street in 1827 in lieu of one in the High Street. Initially this chapel was Presbyterian. OR ZC 1788-1837 (PRO). COP ZC 1788-1837 Mf (WaPL), ZC 1767-1837, B 1758-77 Mf (SRO), Extr C 1788-1837 (IGI).

WALSALL (Lady Hunt Conn), f 1783.

WALSALL (Prim Meth), reg 1830, originally in Hall Lane moving to Townend Bank.

WALSALL (Wes), f 1782, initially in Paradise Court, High Street, moving to Ablewell Street in 1820. OR ZC 1811-37 (PRO), C 1837-1964 (WaPL). COP ZC 1811-37 Mf (SRO, WaPL), Extr C 1811-37 (IGI).

WALSALL Burial Ground, Bath Street. Opened 1756, closed 1855 except for interments in brick vaults and graves. OR B 1756-1857 (WaPL). COP B 1756-1857 (M. Walcot, Holway Ho., Ilminster, Somerset).

WALSALL WOOD St John, erec 1837. Chapelry to St Matthew, Walsall (L). OR C 1835-1904, M 1845-1902, B 1835-1919 (SRO) this includes Ogley Hay C 1840-49.

WALTON. See under BASWICH.

WARLEY (Bapt), Beech Lane. See under WEST BROMWICH.

WARSLOW St James (L), lic 1786. Chapelry to Alstonfield. OR CMB 1785+ (Inc). BT 1786-1800 and 1805-09 given eith Elkstone. COP Extr C 1805-57 (IGI).

WATERFALL St James & St Bartholomew (L) (531). OR C 1602-1859, M 1602-1905, B 1602-1907, Banns 1784-1823 (SRO). BT 1661-1856 (gaps 1685-93, 1776-80, 1845-53) (LJRO). This also contains entries for Calton. COP C 1602-1931, M 1602-1905, B 1602-1907 Ms (WSL, SG, LJRO), Extr C 1661-1856, M 1661-1837 (IGI). See also under CALTON.

WEDNESBURY St Bartholomew (L) (8437). OR CMB 1562+ (gap 1647-63) (Inc). BT 1673-1844 (gaps B 1718, some M 1718, CM 1785-86, part B 1786, 1819, 1821), also including Moxley C 1838-42 (LJRO). COP C 1569-1812, M 1562-1812, B 1561-1812 (gaps 1571-82, B 1580-91) Ms (WSL), CMB 1562-1812 Ms (Homer collection BRL), CMB 1561-1784 p/s (Wednesbury Lib), M 1561-1837 (SMI), Extr C 1813-18, 1820-44, M 1813-36 (IGI).

WEDNESBURY (S of F), reg 1700.

WEDNESBURY (Ind), Hollyhead Road, f 1720.

WEDNESBURY (Prim Meth), Camp Street, erec 1824.

WEDNESBURY (Wes), Spring-head, Spring Bank, f 1760. Note the early registers include Willenhall and possibly Darlaston references. OR ZC 1800-37 (PRO). COP C 1803-37 Mf (WaPL), ZC 1800-37 Mf (SRO), Extr C 1795-1837 (IGI).

WEDNESFIELD St Thomas, erec 1750. Chapelry to Wolverhampton. Royal Peculiar of Wolverhampton. OR C 1751-1974, M 1849-1977, B 1757-1967 (SRO), previous marriages of Wednesfield residents are found in the register of St Peter, Wolverhampton, also C1751-53, 1757-69. BT CB 1799-1835 (gap part 1812) (LJRO). COP CB 1751-1837 (I) ptd (SPRS in conjunction with BMSGH), Extr C 1751-1837 (IGI).

WEDNESFIELD (Wes), erec 1820.

WEEFORD St Mary (L) (470). Peculiar of the Prebend of Alrewas and Weeford. OR CMB 1562+ (Inc). BT 1638-1835 (gaps 1639-83, 1687-89, 1692-96, 1702-04, 1707-10, 1732-35, 1738-44, M 1768-80 listed by SPRS- do not appear) (LJRO). COP CMB 1562-1812 ptd (SPRS), CB 1724-1812, M 1724-53, 1755-1812 p/s (BRL), M 1562-1812 (SMI, CMI), Extr CM 1562-1835 (IGI).

WERRINGTON (Meth NC). See under CAVERSWALL.

WEST BROMWICH All Saints, formerly St Clement (L) (15,327). OR CMB 1608-1975 (SPL). BT 1676-1868 (gaps 1684, 1714, 1735-37, 1829) (LJRO). COP CMB 1608-58 ptd (SPRS), B 1678-1752 Ms (WSL), C 1660-1791, M 1660-1801, B 1660-1777 Ms (WBPL), C 1659-1777, M 1659-1754, B 1658-78 Ms (SG), M 1608-58 (SMI, CMI), Extr C 1608-59, 1678-1828, 1830-68, M 1608-59, 1676-1820, 1830-36 (IGI).

WEST BROMWICH Christ Church, High Street, erec 1829, chapelry to All Saints. OR CMB 1829+ (Inc). BT 1829-35 (LJRO). COP Extr C 1829-35 (IGI).

WEST BROMWICH St Michael (RC), erec 1832. OR C 1832+ M 1834+ (Inc).

WEST BROMWICH (Part Bapt), Providence Chapel, Sandwell Road, erec 1810.

WEST BROMWICH (Bapt), Dartmouth Street, erec 1835. Another at Beech Lane, Warley, erec 1825.

WEST BROMWICH (Ind), Ebenezer Chapel formerly the Old Meeting House, Carters Green, f 1662. OR ZC 1803-36, B 1835-36 (PRO). COP ZC 1803-37, B 1837 Mf (SRO), Extr C 1803-37 (IGI).

WEST BROMWICH (Ind), Mayers Green, Messenger Lane, f 1785. This chapel was used by the Countess of Huntingdon's Connexion from 1785 to 1800. OR C 1787-1837 (PRO). COP ZC 1787-1837 Mf (SRO), Extr C 1787-1837 (IGI).

WEST BROMWICH (Lady Hunt Conn), Hill Top, Dudley Street, reg 1751. A chapel was erected in 1785, moving to Messenger Lane in 1787, which latter chapel became an Independent chapel in 1800. For OR see under WEST BROMWICH (Ind).

WEST BROMWICH (Meth NC), Victoria Street, erec 1824. Moved to Junction Street about 1851.

WEST BROMWICH (Prim Meth), erec 1831. Another at Union Street, erec 1833, another at Greets (or Gold) Green, erec 1836 and another at Lyne, erec 1834.

WEST BROMWICH (Wes), Meeting Street, f 1760. OR ZC 1815-37, B 1837 (PRO). COP ZC 1815-37 (SRO), Extr C 1815-37 (IGI).

WEST BROMWICH (Wes), Victoria Street, erec 1830, another at High Street, erec 1835, another at Greets Green, erec 1834, another at Hill Top, erec 1831, and another at Lyne, erec 1834.

WESTON-UNDER-LIZARD St Andrew (L) (257). OR C 1701-1933, M 1701-1853, B 1701-1805, Banns 1754-1812 (SRO). BT 1660-1865 (gaps 1698-1701, 1710-14, 1786-91, 1836-61) (LJRO). COP CMB 1654-1812 (I) ptd (SPRS), M 1654-1812 (SMI, CMI), Extr C 1653-1812, 1814-65, M 1657-1812, 1814-33 (IGI), M 1634-1837 (SMI).

WESTON UPON TRENT St Andrew (L) (608). OR C 1538-1903, M 1538-1837, B 1538-1899 (SRO). BT 1666-1862 (gaps 1741-44, CB 1758-62, 1839) (LJRO). COP Extr C 1666-1741, 1744-1864, M 1744-1859 (IGI).

WESTON UPON TRENT (Ind), reg 1817.

WETLEY ROCKS St John, erec 1833. Chapelry to Cheddleton (L). OR CMB ?1834+ (Inc). BT 1835-68 (gaps 1853, 1857) (LJRO). COP Extr C 1834-68 (IGI).

WETLEY ROCKS (Ind), reg 1821. Probably closed before 1850.

WETTON St Margaret (L) (497). OR C 1657-1813, M 1657-1812, B 1657-1813, Banns 1823-1851 (SRO), CMB 1813+ (INc). BT 1660-1869 (gaps 1698-1701, 1708-11, 1755-58, CB 1776-80, 1838) (LJRO). COP C (BT) 1841-69 (IGI).

WETTON (Ind), reg 1811.

WETTON (Wes), erec 1828.

WHEATON ASTON, chapelry to Lapley, erec before 1800 (L). Entries are included with Lapley (q.v.).

WHEATON ASTON (Ind), Zion Chapel, f 1806.

WHEATON ASTON (Prim Meth), erec 1832.

WHICHNOR. See under WICHNOR.

WHISTON, Kingsley. See under KINGSLEY.

WHISTON, Penkridge. See under PENKRIDGE.

WHITEHOUGH (S of F). See under IPSTONES.

WHITMORE St Mary & All Saints (L) (281). Chapelry to Trentham. OR C 1558-1957, M 1754-1964, B 1813-98 (SRO). BT 1674-1838 (gaps 1676-80, 1747-55, 1795-1805, 1836-37) (LJRO), the period from 1754 to 1801 contains some Stoke marriages.

WHITTINGTON St Giles (L) (773). Peculiar of Whittington and Baswich. OR CMB 1574+ (Inc). BT 1663-1870 (gaps 1686-92, 1702-04, 1707-10, 1721-24, 1735-38, 1741-44, 1762-65, 1796-98, 1816, M 1841-70, CB 1858, 1868) (LJRO). COP Extr C 1663-1870, M 1663-1812 (IGI).

WICHNOR St Leonard (L). Chapelry to Tatenhill until 1881. OR CB 1731-1812, M 1755-1804, 1813-1836 (SRO), CB 1812+ M 1837+ (Inc). BT 1660-1864 (gap 1836-63) (LJRO). COP Extr C 1660-63, 1674-1835 (IGI).

WIGGINTON St Leonard, erec 1777, chapelry to Tamworth (L). No registers. See under TAMWORTH.

WILLENHALL St Giles (L). Chapelry to Wolverhampton St Peter. Royal Peculiar of Wolverhampton. OR CMB 1642+ (Inc), C 1724-27 with Wolverhampton St Peter. BT 1799-1825 (marriages in Wolverhampton) (LJRO). COP CB 1642-1812 (I) Ms (WSL), C 1642-1812, B 1727-1812 (I) Ms (SG Pink Linen S), C 1642-1812 Ms (LJRO), Vestry Minute Book Ms (SG, SRO), Extr C 1799-1825 (IGI).

WILLENHALL (Part Bapt), Little London, reg 1787.

WILLENHALL (Ind), reg 1821.

WILLENHALL (Wes), Union Street, f 1805. OR Register for Springhead, Wednesbury includes some Willenhall references.

WILLENHALL (Wes), erec 1833. OR Register for Springhead, Wednesbury includes some Willenhall references.

WILLENHALL (Wes), Portabello, erec 1836. OR C 1850-91 (WaPL). The register for Spring-head, Wednesbury includes some Willenhall references.

WILNECOTE Holy Trinity (L), transferred to Staffs in 1964. OR CMB 1763+ (Inc). BT 1857-62 (gap 1858-59) (LJRO). COP C 1763-83 Mf (tamworth Mf SRO).

WOLSTANTON St Margaret (L) (10,853). OR C 1628-1966, M 1628-1953, B 1628-1952 (SRO). BT 1662-1881 (gaps 1668-72, 1721, 1763-65, M 1826, 1827, 1838)) (LJRO). COP CMB 1624-1812 (I) ptd (SPRS), M 1624-1812 (SMI, CMI), Extr C 1624-1875, M 1674-1825, 1828-37 (IGI). See also under KIDSGROVE, NEWCHAPEL and TUNSTALL.

WOLSTANTON (S of F), Knutton, f 1672. Member of Leek MM.

WOLSTANTON (Meth NC), Providence Chapel, erec 1828.

WOLSTANTON (Prim Meth), erec 1830, another at Chell, erec 1823, another at Chesterton, erec 1834.

.WOLSTANTON (Wes), erec 1830. OR Baptismal entries may be included in the Circuit register for which see under BURSLEM, Swan Bank.

WOLSTANTON (Wes), Chesterton, erec before 1800. OR Baptisms for Wolstanton chapels may be included in the Circuit rgister for which see under BURSLEM, Swan Bank.

WOLSTANTON (Wes), Golden Hill, erec 1822, another at Harriseahead, erec 1801 and another at Knutton Heath, erec 1824. The latter has extant C 1841-75 (NPL). For earlier baptisms, entries may be found in the Circuit register for which see under BURSLEM, Swan Bank.

WOLVERHAMPTON St Peter (L) (48,183). Royal Peculiar of Wolverhampton. OR C 1603-1897, M 1603-1851, B 1603-1862, Banns 1845-60 (SRO). Includes some Willenhall and Wednesfield baptisms (SRO). BT 1799-1833 including Bilston marr. (LJRO). COP CMB 1539-1660 (I) extr only until 1603 ptd (SPRS), M

1660-1776 ptd (SPRS), C 1660-1733, 1776-98, M 1776-98, B 1670-1731/2 (LJRO), CMB 1603-60, M 1776-1836 Ms (WoPL), CMB 1784-1839 (I for M 1813-37) Ms (WSL), Extr CMB 1654-1751 (BRL), Churchwardens Account Book 1519-1638 (SRO), M 1660-1776 (SMI), M 1539-1776 (CMI-Wolverhampton), Extr C 1542-1660, 1799-1844, M 1538-1652, 1661-1734, 1799-1830 (IGI).

WOLVERHAMPTON St John. An Act was passed in 1755 but due to a fire, not completed until 1776. OR included in St Peter's up to 1840.

WOLVERHAMPTON St George, Bilston Street, erec 1830. Royal Peculiar of Wolverhampton. OR 1834-1977, M 1834-1976, B 1834-1937 (SRO). BT None.

WOLVERHAMPTON St Paul, Penn Road, erec 1835. OR CMB 1835+ (Inc). BT None. See also under BILSTON, PELSALL, WEDNESFIELD and WILLENHALL.

WOLVERHAMPTON St Peter & St Paul, North Street (RC), erec c.1750. OR C 1791-1910, fragmentary notes of C 1754-91, M 1837-54, D 1784-1911, Easter communicants 1809-44 in Baptismal register, plan of burial ground (Inc). COP C 1788-1830, B 1784-1828 ptd (SPRS), CB 1784-1839 Ms (WoPL), M 1788-1848 (SMI), Extr C 1736-45, 1759-73, 1788-1830 (IGI).

WOLVERHAMPTON (S of F), Canal Street.

WOLVERHAMPTON (Part Bapt), Old Baptist Chapel, Temple Street, erec 1785. Formerly, Temple Street was called Grey Peak Walk.

WOLVERHAMPTON (Bapt), Walsall Street, f 1829. OR Z & namings 1832-37 (PRO). COP Z 1832-37 Mf (SRO), Extr Z 1832-37 (IGI).

WOLVERHAMPTON (Ind), Temple Street formerly Grey Pea Walk, f 1770. The Temple Street chapel was vacated and the members joined the Snow Hill Congregational Church about 1849. OR ZC 1771-1836, B 1787-99 (PRO), CM 1849-64 (Snow Hill Chapel) (WoPL). COP C 1782-1836, B 1786-99 Mf (SRO), Extr C 1771-1836 (IGI).

WOLVERHAMPTON (Ind), Queen Street (erec 1813), formerly Princes Street (erec 1804), and formerly Pountreys Fold (f 1780). OR ZC 1785-1836 (PRO). COP ZC 1785-1836 Mf (SRO), Extr C 1785-99, 1809-36 (IGI).

WOLVERHAMPTON (Pres), John Street, f 1692, chapel occupied by Part Bapts in 1851. OR ZC 1726-1815 (PRO). COP C 1726-39, 1759-1815, D 1726-29 Mf (SRO), Extr C 1726-38, 1760-1815 (IGI).

WOLVERHAMPTON (Pres), Snow Hill Chapel, f 1700, later joined Temple St Ind. OR ZC 1830-38 (PRO), CM 1849-64 (Ind) (WoPL). COP ZC 1830-38 Mf (SRO), Extr C 1830-38 (IGI).

WOLVERHAMPTON (Pres), Trinity Presbyterian Chapel, Cleveland Street, erec 1836.

WOLVERHAMPTON (Lady Hunt Conn), f 1782.

WOLVERHAMPTON (Meth NC), Mount Zion Chapel, Horsley Fields, erec 1829.

WOLVERHAMPTON (Prim Meth), Duke Street, erec 1833.

WOLVERHAMPTON (Wes), Darlington Street, f 1793. Originally met in Noah's Arc, reg 1793, which seceeded to John Street Presb. Darlington Street chapel erec 1825. OR ZC 1793-1820, 1793-1837 (PRO), C 1793-1856, M 1878+ (WoPL), C 1857+ (Inc). COP ZC 1793-1820, 1793-1837 (SRO), Extr C 1787-1837 (IGI).

WOLVERHAMPTON (Wes), reg 1826.

WOLVERHAMPTON, Shooters Hill, Mount Zion, reg 1809. No denomination was given for this registration.

WOMBOURNE St Benedict (L) (1647). OR CMB 1570-1812 (SRO), CMB 1813+ (Inc). BT 1655-1856 (gaps 1662-63, 1693-98, 1730-32, M 1766-76, M 1791-1800, 1813,

1816, 1841-42, 1853-55) (LJRO). COP C 1570-79, 1798-1812, MB 1570-1812 Mf (SRO), CMB 1570-1725 Ms (WSL), Extr C 1655-1812, 1814-56, M 1655-1766, M 1776-86, 1800-12, 1814-48 (IGI).

WOMBOURNE (Ind), erec 1837.

WOMBOURNE (Ind), Ebenezer Chapel, Swindon, erec 1820.

WOORE St Leionrd, chapelry to Mucklestone. Now in Salop. OR C 1831+ MB 1842+ (Inc). BT 1831-58 included with Mucklestone for years 1758-79, 1786-91, 1797-1800, 1803-05, 1807-09 (LJRO). COP C 1769-1808 (WSL with Mucklestone), Extr C 1769-1804 (IGI listed under Salop).

WOORE (Prim Meth), erec 1833.

WORDSLEY Holy Trinity, erec 1831. When this church was erected it assumed the role of the Kingswinford parish church from St Mary's, whose registers were transferred and continued at Holy Trinity. Thus the early Kingswinford registers are often listed under Holy Trinity. OR C 1603-1945, M 1603-1958, B 1603-1927 (DPL). BT 1832-54 (LJRO). COP Extr C 1832-45 (IGI).

WORDSLEY (Ind), f 1808, associated with High Street Ind Chapel, Stourbridge, Worcs (OR's at PRO) until 1819.

WRYLEY GREAT. See under NORTON CANES.

WYNCHOR. See under WICHNOR.

YOXALL St Petr (L) (1582). OR C 1645-1786, 1813-1909. M 1682-1915, B 1678-1879, Banns 1823-83 (SRO). BT 1664-1871 (gaps 1665-67, 1676, 1701, 1705-07, 1771-81, 1870) (LJRO). COP C 1644-1726, M 1682-1754 Ms (SG Pink Linen), Extr CM 1666-1770, 1782-1856 (IGI).

YOXALL St Francis (RC), Wood Lane. OR C 1797-1842, M 1841+ (Inc). COP C 1797+ Ms (DA).

YOXALL (RC), Hoarcross Hall, reg 1791. This belonged to the Howard family for many generations. In 1793 the property was sold and the mission was transferred to Wood Lane.

YOXALL (Prim Meth), Mount Zion, Wood Lane, erec 1822.

B'ham + Midlan
Soc for Genealogy +
Heral
£3.40